D1341824

MY STORY

How Love Changed Everything

COLIN THACKERY
MY STORY
How Love Changed Everything

C

An Hachette UK Company
www.hachette.co.uk

First published in Great Britain in 2019 by Cassell,
an imprint of Octopus Publishing Group Ltd
Carmelite House
50 Victoria Embankment
London EC4Y 0DZ
www.octopusbooks.co.uk

Copyright © Thackerafies Limited 2019

All rights reserved. No part of this work may be reproduced or
utilized in any form or by any means, electronic or mechanical,
including photocopying, recording or by any information
storage and retrieval system, without the prior written
permission of the publisher.

Colin Thackery asserts the moral right to be identified
as the author of this work.

ISBN 978-1-78840-224-8

A CIP catalogue record for this book is available from
the British Library.

Printed and bound in the United Kingdom.
1 3 5 7 9 10 8 6 4 2

Writer: Christian Guiltenane

Publishing Director: Trevor Davies
Senior Designer: Jaz Bahra
Typesetter: Jeremy Tilston
Senior Editor: Sarah Reece
Copy Editor: Muna Reyal
Senior Production Manager: Peter Hunt

The Scarlet coat is a registered trademark
of the Royal Hospital Chelsea.

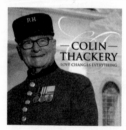

Colin's album is available now. Tickets for his tour
are available from gigsandtours.com

For Joan

Contents

Prologue

It has to be one of the most extraordinary moments of my entire life. There I am, standing on a stage in front of thousands of people and millions of TV viewers, being told that the nation has voted me their favourite act on *Britain's Got Talent* 2019. Gold confetti is raining down on me and the screaming and applause emanating from the audience is rather deafening and incredibly overwhelming. This wasn't what I had expected when I applied to go on the show all those months ago. It was all a bit of a lark to start with, but then, bizarrely, I appeared to be doing well and made it past my first audition, then through the semifinals and – unbelievably – to the grand finale, where 12 acts had fought it out to win not only £250,000, but also, more excitingly for me, the chance to perform for royalty at the prestigious Royal Variety Performance.

By rights, none of this should have happened to me. In March 2020 I turn 90 years old. Who has ever heard of an 89-year-old winner of a reality talent show? Normally these shows are set up to discover fresh young talent with the view of developing them into a hugely successful global star. But I'm 89. I have had two heart attacks, am not the most agile fella around and I have no interest in falling out of nightclubs or being surrounded by groupies. In some ways I feel as if this experience shouldn't be mine. Except that it is. I released my first album, *Love Changes Everything*, at the age of 89. On my 90th birthday in March 2020 I will be on tour, singing to audiences around the UK. In fact, folks, I'm now thinking life actually begins at 90. Which is amazing considering almost three years ago I thought my life had come to an end when I lost my darling wife, Joan, after 66 years of marriage. When she died in my arms, my world collapsed around me. The woman who had inspired me to reach for the stars was no longer there. For a time, I couldn't imagine a life without her. I saw no future, no reason to carry on. The prospect of living life on my own without someone to love was utterly heartbreaking.

But then the smothering fog of mourning somewhat disappeared, and I remembered that I have two wonderful children, four gorgeous grandchildren and Joan, rooting for me every step of the way. Yes, Joan may have passed, but she is still part of my life. I love her just as much as I did when she was by my side – and I know she loves me. She tells me so, when I sit in my room at the Royal Hospital Chelsea. I look at the picture that hangs opposite my bed and we chat. I keep Joan alive in my heart and, through all the processes of *BGT*, she was there, standing in front of me. Every song I sang was for Joan. She was, she is, the wind beneath my wings, and I remember all so clearly that first day she danced into my life…

PART 1

The girl who won my heart

CHAPTER 1

Our first dance

There was something about you, Joan, that was simply extra-ordinary, something magical about you that drew my eye and held my gaze for longer than I probably should have allowed it to.

Unlike the rest of the lovely local lasses who came to dance to the latest big band sounds, you practically oozed what I would confidently describe as class and sophistication. You looked a little younger and more refined than most of your peers, but you possessed the air of a woman who knew exactly who she was and understood the world she lived in.

Most importantly, though, you were a right little stunner. There was no doubt about that! You were the most beautiful girl in the room, if not the village of Willington. Heck, I would even go so far as to say you were the best-looking lass in the whole of County Durham. You were dressed immaculately in a fashionable frock that showcased your trim figure, and your bright and inviting face was framed charmingly by dark wavy locks that fell just above your shoulder. Your pale skin shimmered in the light, giving your large dark eyes and gentle red lips more of a platform to shine.

To say I was enchanted was an understatement. I simply couldn't tear my eyes away from you, even if I wanted to. Not that I did, mind. Better still, you were looking straight at me with a smile across your lips.

Without a moment's hesitation, I confidently started across the floor, ready to sweep you off your feet and enchant you with my best dance moves. But, before I could reach you, a distracted couple waltzed straight into me, almost knocking me off my feet. The delay cost me dearly because by the time I had settled myself, a fella had beaten me to you and was already dancing with you.

I was devastated, but not defeated. There was no way I was giving up that easily. And by the way you kept glancing at me with your coy smile, as you were spun around and around by my dance rival, I knew my moment was still to come.

The year was 1949. Remember Joan? I was fresh to the area, having just been transferred from the Royal Artillery band in Salisbury. Aged just 15, I had joined the Army Boys' Service, where I had spent several years before being recruited and touring extensively across the world with the RA band. My father, who was also in the Army, had had words with certain officials and demanded that I transfer to regimental service to further my career. As a result, I was posted up north to join 700 other fellas at the new camp, Brancepeth, near Willington. It was a camp for both the Durham and Duke of Wellington's Light Infantry regiments. And I was positively thrilled about it.

You'll remember, I absolutely loved being part of the Army. It had been a dream of mine to become a soldier for as long as I could remember (well, at least once I'd realised I was never going to become a cowboy) and it had provided me with a life far removed from the glum, chaotic childhood I had led in grotty post-Great Depression, pre-war London, the memories of which still filled me with a chilly sadness.

But that felt like a hundred years ago. I was relieved to have broken free from the squalor and sad neglect of my home life, and I had heartily thrown myself into a new life as a soldier and band member.

No sooner had I settled into my new barracks than I had been delighted to discover that there was going to be a big dance held at the camp on the Thursday and that girls from the local area would be in attendance. What a way to mark my arrival, I remember thinking to myself. I really did love dancing, mainly because I had learned to dance as a youngster.

You see, back in London, when I was around 14 – a time of doing without, when I inexplicably used to draw a flamboyant moustache above my top lip with Mother's mascara – I had attended a tiny dance school at the top of Camden High Street and learned all of the popular dances of the time, such as the foxtrot, the tango, the quick step and the waltz – you know, all the dances you see nowadays on *Strictly Come Dancing*. Music had always been a love of mine and I enjoyed big band jazz most of all, so whenever I heard it, you'd more than likely catch me dancing to it.

The dance classes – which I paid for myself using funds earned via various, not-always legal methods – were fun and I relished every minute of them, even though the lads I hung out with on the streets didn't understand why I enjoyed dancing so. But I didn't care what they thought about it. Don't get me wrong, I wasn't the leader of the pack or anything, none of us were. But I was forthright and wasn't afraid to stand my ground if someone tried to make trouble.

But I digress. Let's get back to the matter at hand – the dance and, yes, meeting you, Joan.

Before I had headed off to the camp dance that evening, I had taken time to prepare myself because I wanted to make a good impression, slipping into my uniform and making sure it was spick and span. Not only would girls from the local villages be in attendance, but so, too, would be the young wives and daughters of my fellow soldiers who lived in the married quarters. I strode into the dance hall a little after 7.30, decked out in all my military best, feeling very confident indeed. Invincible, perhaps.

And that's when I saw you for the first time.

But with you now being swept around the floor by a rival, I knew I had to act; either to focus my attention on winning you over or simply to bail out. Well, I was no quitter, that's for sure, so I threw myself into the group dances on the floor, dazzling the other girls and the disgruntled lads with my moves, but always keeping a keen eye on you. I remember being impressed that you were a whizz on the floor, which made you all the more attractive. 'She is the one for me,' I whispered to myself, unable to take my eyes off you. 'I must get a dance with her.'

Events like this were usually hosted by a fella you'd call a dance leader, who would announce what the next style would be. This was the chance for lads like me to cut in and ask a girl for a dance. These were called 'excuse me' dances, and while a chap with a soft spot for a girl might be a tad disappointed to lose her to another dance partner, it was just the way the cookie crumbled and no feathers were ruffled.

Throughout the night there were various 'spot dances', where couples could win a prize if they landed on the right spot when the music came to an end. But the most fun dance of all was the barn dance. This was a hoot and it gave everyone the perfect opportunity to meet each other mid-routine. The boys would form a circle on the outside while the girls would gather inside. When the music began to play, the boys would move in one direction and the girls in the other. When the music stopped, the girl standing opposite you would be your next partner.

Determined to dance with you, I did everything I possibly could to ensure I ended up as the lucky fella standing opposite you, spinning my various 'temporary' partners around the floor a little too fast to ensure that I put myself in prime position to finally meet you.

Lo and behold, my plan actually worked and you were soon standing right there in front of me. Without any time to exchange niceties, the pair of us took off around the floor as if we had danced together a thousand times. Up close, you were even prettier than I had thought, and those eyes! As we covered the floor, the world around me felt as though it was melting away again and I could feel something between us, something magnetic. I knew for certain that this was going to be the start of something very special indeed.

At the end of the dance, we simply stared at each other as we got our breath back and then we laughed, which broke the ice. This was looking good, I remember thinking to myself. Mission almost accomplished! However, when I asked you if I could have the next tango, you simply laughed and replied with a knowing smile and a gently raised eyebrow, 'How many other girls have you asked?' I was taken aback at first. You were certainly sassy, that's for sure, and I couldn't help but admire the fact that you were playing hard to get. But before I could utter one of my disarmingly witty ripostes, you suddenly turned on your heel and walked off the floor, just like Cinderella, to God-knows-where. I was absolutely heartbroken. This hadn't gone the way I'd expected it to. But I wasn't going to give up!

After a thorough search of the hall, I realised you'd gone so I reluctantly spent the remaining hours dancing with the other girls, though not one of them compared to you.

When the evening came to an end, I strolled back to camp, with a heavy heart and my hands buried deep in my pockets. As I retired to my bunk, all I could think about was you. But little did I know then that the girl I had met that evening would be the one to change my life forever.

CHAPTER 2

Falling in love

Joan and I had been married for 66 years when she died in December 2016, but even though I know she is no longer physically with me, she still lives on in my mind and heart. Every morning and every night I sit on the edge of my bed in my berth at the Royal Hospital, staring at the portrait of my beautiful Joan that hangs on the wall, telling her what I have been up to which, admittedly, has been rather a lot since my appearance on *Britain's Got Talent*. Some people might think it odd that I still speak to someone who is no longer there. Some people might think I'm quite mad. But I'm far from it. You see, I loved Joan all of my adult life and I wasn't ready to lose her when I did on that cold winter's day. While I have, over time, come to terms with the heartbreaking realization that Joan is no longer by my side, I am at my happiest when I am conversing with her and telling her over and over again that I love her now just as much as I ever did. Does she reply to me? Yes, I like to think she does. For almost 70 years we were barely apart, so I think I can imagine what she would want to say to me.

Joan was a wonderful wife. She was my support and anchor, who gave me the best years of my life. Not only did she bless me with two beautiful children, Dawn and Peter, but she is also, quite frankly, the reason I am the man I am today. Every step of the way, she was there, offering encouragement, lifting my spirits when they were low, giving me the love I dearly needed given the experience of my childhood. She truly made me believe that anything was possible, that if I reached for the stars, there was nothing in the world that could stop me from fulfilling my dreams. As clichéd as it sounds, she was indeed the wind beneath my wings.

To think that I almost lost her that night back in 1949 doesn't bear thinking about. It might sound like this was merely an intense infatuation with a pretty girl I'd just met, but that first encounter on the dance floor was really quite something and made rather a big impression on my heart. For some reason, I truly believed – and please don't ask me how – that I had met the woman whom I would be with for the rest of my life, even if she had given me the brush-off in the most spectacular of ways. But I still believed, as unlikely as it might have seemed, that one day soon we would meet again.

In the days that followed our first encounter, my mind was all of a dither, thinking only about that girl. Although it felt like she had won my heart, I didn't really know a single thing about her, except that her name was Joan, she was breathtakingly beautiful, a local lass and an impeccable dancer. I was determined to find out more, but it all depended on whether our paths would cross again. Luckily, there was another dance planned for the following Thursday so I had everything crossed that I would bump into her again. But before then I had to concentrate on life at the camp.

I had only been in County Durham a short while before I met Joan. Prior to that I had travelled the world with the Royal Artillery band and before that I had spent my formative years working hard and learning the military ropes with the Royal Artillery at the Boys' Battery in the Woolwich Barracks in London. That's where young fellas like me get knocked into shape so that one day they can stand proud and fight for their country, something that I really hoped to do.

My father, Sergeant Major Albert Thackery, of whom I will speak more later, was stationed with the Royal Engineers in London and had not been happy that I was gallivanting around the world with the Royal Artillery band. Father told me later that he was concerned that there was little chance of progression for me there and was keen to see me do well and flourish within the military. He went straight to the director of music, who had originally plucked me from Boys' Service, and demanded that I return to duty and back to a unit. At first, the musical director apparently dug his heels in and refused to let me go, but then Father told him in no uncertain terms, 'I'm entitled to claim him into the Royal Engineers.' He was right. Parents who were in the military had the power to do just that – so that is how I found myself moving to 45th Field Regiment at Brancepeth Camp in County Durham.

Brancepeth was a lovely-looking camp. Well, nicer than most, probably because it was attached to a rather magnificent-looking castle that dated back to medieval times. I remember getting off the train, walking along the straight road towards the castle and seeing the impressive pile come into view. I don't think I'd seen anything quite like it before, with its tall medieval towers and imposing structure. It was the kind of place you saw in history books and was nothing like I was used to seeing on the streets of Camden, where I'd grown up for the first 14 years of my life.

On arrival I was assigned to 70 Battery, to be trained as a technical assistant. This meant working in the command post, which is the room where artillery-gun firing is controlled. I was allotted a bed space in a long hut with 11 other chaps. This type of camp was known as a spider camp, due to the ablution block being in the middle of the accommodation blocks – the set up looked like a spider from above. The blokes I was bunking with all seemed pleasant enough, but none particularly stood out to me to start with. I was very much a fella who liked his own company, so was not in the habit of being too friendly. Later on I did develop friendships with Ken Brown and Sefton Smith, who I got to know better throughout my time in the army and beyond but, as always in life, these relationships took a time to form.

As the first week drifted by, I began to get a good feel for the camp and felt suitably settled – my handful of years at Boys' Service and then touring ensured I felt at home wherever I was. I also gradually became somewhat intrigued by a rather odd fella called Sefton Smith, upon whom my superiors had asked me to keep an eye because he appeared so haphazard. He was an odd chap, for sure. To look at him, you would think he was incapable of caring for himself. But, as I was soon to find out, there was more to him than met the eye.

For one reason or another, the rest of our barracks had packed up and disappeared home on the first weekend of our stay, leaving just Sefton and me to potter around the cavernous camp as if we were the last souls on earth. It really was a different place when there wasn't a brigade of other guys about. It felt like a silent empty shell, with just the sound of the clock ticking hypnotically and the blustery winter winds howling away outside. Keen to avoid slipping into a boredom-induced coma, I hopped on the edge of Sefton's bunk and suggested we go for a drink somewhere. 'Yes please,' he replied enthusiastically, tossing aside the book he'd been reading for hours, 'We need to do something because this place is like a morgue.'

Chuckling away at our predicament, we slipped into our uniform, jumped on a bus and headed for the centre of the nearby village, Willington. There we stumbled upon a rather homely little pub that was packed to the rafters with locals downing drinks and having a good old singsong. However, as we stepped over the hearth, clad in our battledress, every head turned to stare at us and the chatter suddenly ceased, just like in the Westerns I used to watch as a youngster. Sefton and I gave each other an awkward side glance, worried for a moment that we might not be welcome in this place. But when the revellers burst into joyful banter and ushered us to the bar, offering us free drink upon drink, our fears were wonderfully allayed.

As we settled in for a night of high jinks, one of the burly locals banged solidly on a table and demanded that someone step up to the piano for a singsong. Sefton and I looked around the room to see which of our new comrades would be brave enough to volunteer, totally oblivious to the fact that the fella already had his eyes fixed on us. 'Lad, he's talking about you,' someone piped up, giving me a firm nudge in the ribs. 'Yes, you soldier lads, come over here and give us a song,' the first fella bellowed.

Now, as you know, I do love a rousing sing-a-long so we heartily agreed.

As we wriggled our way through the crowd to take our positions, Sefton whispered under his breath that he was able to play the piano 'a little bit', so we decided that I would sing and he would try to follow me on the ol' Joanna!

But as we soon as we launched into a series of rousing old Cockney favourites that I used to sing back home with my grandfather, Grandad Tom, I was surprised to discover that Sefton's performance levels were really quite extraordinary! He wasn't just an adequate player, haphazardly bluffing his way around the keys like a novice, he sounded like an absolute professional. I was really quite astonished. The folks in the pub also appeared impressed by our talents and became so enthralled by our joyful double act that they insisted we carried on belting out songs until last orders, rewarding us with free beers all night before sending us off, back to camp, feeling a little worse for wear. Years later, in Korea, I would perform with Sefton again, in the Army's concert party.

The Thursday following our night out was the evening I met Joan for the first time and, a week on from that, I was desperately hopeful that I would see her again at the next organized dance.

This time round, I knew I had to impress her properly so that she would take me seriously. I didn't just want to dance with her, I wanted to get to know her better. But from what she'd said to me on the night – *'How many other girls have you asked?'* – I was aware she thought I was some kind of fancy-footed Casanova, which couldn't have been further from the truth. This meant I had my work cut out.

As I got ready for my night out, I took extra care over my appearance, making sure my face was well scrubbed, my teeth clean and my breath minty fresh. Sefton gave me a final once-over, straightening my crooked shirt collar and dusting down my jacket.

When I arrived at the dance, the place was packed out with soldiers and lasses spinning each other around the floor to the jaunty tunes performed by the house band.

A cursory glance around the room left me disappointed as I could see no sign of Joan whatsoever and I suddenly feared the worst. What if she wasn't coming? What if she had moved away? What if she was missing the dance altogether just to avoid bumping into me again? As a hundred more excuses for her absence cascaded through my head, Joan appeared suddenly, as if out of nowhere. Without wasting a precious moment, I weaved my way through the spinning couples on the dance floor to introduce myself properly.

'Good evening Miss,' I ventured, trying to be heard over the big band sounds blaring away in the background. 'My name is Thackery. Colin Thackery. Pleased to meet you properly.'

Joan flashed me a smile and held out her hand. 'I'm Joan. Nice to see you. Again.'

Her hand felt soft between my fingers and I held onto it for perhaps a little too long, muttering, 'I'm terribly sorry if I offended you.'

'I beg your pardon?' she asked, leaning in close.

I repeated myself, just as the band played its last note and right before the crowd burst into gleeful applause. 'I'm sorry if I offended you.' This time, the words came out loud and clear, pricking the ears of the lads and lasses in our vicinity, who looked over to work out what I had done so wrong before getting swept into the applause.

'Don't be silly,' she replied in her soft Durham accent. 'You have nothing to say sorry for.'

A tsunami of excitement instantly surged through me. This was going better than I thought. For one, she hadn't scarpered, and secondly, she appeared not to bear any ill feeling towards me after last week's episode.

Before she had a chance to change her mind, I eagerly asked her to dance and, before I knew it, we were waltzing away like Fred and Ginger. Occasionally we took a breather from the floor, and we talked and talked as the rest of the world carried on around us. She told me about her job as a milliner at Wilkinson, a large drapers and ladies and gentlemen's outfitters in Bishop Auckland, how she was one of eight siblings and how her war-veteran dad would frown upon our union because of his belief that soldiers were no good for any daughter of his.

When the night came to an end, my heart sank. Having spent the entire night with Joan, I simply didn't want it to end. But, as I walked her to the bus stop, I realised this was just the beginning and that I should be patient and let things grow naturally. I knew from the first moment I saw her that there was something special about Joan, but this night had cemented my feelings. I was in love – not just infatuated, but in love, as silly as it sounds.

Of course, I dared not say anything yet, for fear I'd scare the lass off, but I sensed, as we waited hand in hand at the bus stop, that Joan was feeling the same way. When we looked at each other, it was with an intensity I had never experienced before, as if we were trying to memorize everything about each other's faces for our mind's eye to store until we next saw each other. As the bus headlights appeared along the road and its growling engine grew louder and louder, my heart sank, knowing we didn't have long until we had to say goodbye. Once again, we looked into each other's eyes.

'There's another dance in Willington on Saturday...' Joan ventured. 'I'm not sure what you're doing that night, but I was, er, thinking of going.'

I chuckled. 'I wouldn't miss it for the world.'

As the bus pulled up to the stop, I leaned in and planted a light kiss on her cheek. 'Goodnight sweetheart,' I said, looking like a Cheshire cat that had lapped up all the cream. 'I'll see you at the bus stop. Saturday! Seven o'clock sharp!'

As Joan climbed aboard the bus and took her seat by a window, I suddenly felt a pang of sheer devastation grip my heart, the kind of ache you experience when you lose or break a treasured possession. The pain grew stronger as the bus eased away and headed off into the darkness of night. I waited until I could see its tail-lights no more and then began to mooch my way back to camp with my head full of memories. It was only then, when I was alone, that I realised just how bitterly cold it was.

CHAPTER 3

A secret romance

O nce again, the week drifted by too slowly for my liking but, when Saturday finally arrived, I made sure I was at the bus stop extra early to meet Joan. I didn't know why, but I'd convinced myself that it was a much better idea to be pacing up and down in the freezing cold than sitting in the warmer barracks.

When the bus arrived, just after seven, I could see Joan sitting solemnly by the window, with her hair hanging down across one side of her face. I waved at her like a maniac, excited to see her again. But when she stepped off the bus, she seemed somewhat reserved. Had something changed? As I approached her, she turned her head away, clearly trying to avoid my gaze.

'What's wrong?' I asked, worried that the flame I thought she was carrying for me was all but extinguished.

'Nothing,' she sighed dismissively, walking on ahead.

'There's *something*,' I pleaded. 'I just know it.' I reached for her arm but she wriggled free.

Joan carried on walking until I called out her name. She stopped still, but didn't turn.

'What's wrong?' I asked resting my hands on her shoulders from behind. 'Is it me? Is it something I've done?'

'No,' she replied, starting to turn towards me. 'It's something *I've* done.'

Having fully turned to me, she pulled back the hair that was draped over one side of her face to reveal a massive purple and yellow bruise that surrounded a rather squished-looking eye. I gasped out loud. It was the worst shiner I had ever seen in my life.

'What the hell...?' I began, concerned that some bounder had hurt her. 'Who did this? I swear, I'll sort them out if you tell me who did this to you.'

Joan giggled momentarily. 'Oh Colin, you are a sweetheart,' she said, more upbeat than I expected her to sound. 'It was just an accident. I was playing netball with the girls and all of a sudden someone elbowed me right in the eye. It hurt like mad at the time, but it looks worse than it feels now.'

I wrapped my arms around her and gave her a gentle squeeze. 'Oh Joan,' I breathed into her ear, enjoying the unexpected intimacy. 'What are we going to do with you, eh?'

I laughed and so, too, did Joan.

'But we can't go to the dance,' she carried on.

'Why not? I've been looking forward to it all week,' I said.

'I can't go looking like this! I'd never live it down,' she argued. 'Everyone will stare at me.'

'Who cares?' I hit back, worried that she might want to head home again. 'Let them stare. That nasty old bruise hasn't made you any less beautiful. In fact, I think it makes you look even prettier.'

Joan flashed me an unconvinced look and then creased up into laughter.

'I've been looking forward to seeing you all week,' I pleaded. 'I don't want to go back to the camp.'

'Who said anything about going home, you great fool,' she laughed. 'I'm not going home, I'm just saying I can't go to the dance looking like I've done ten rounds in a boxing ring.'

Instead, we decided to go for a walk, got some chips from the chippie and chatted the night away, hardly pausing for breath.

At the end of the night, we agreed to meet again at the camp dance the following week and again at the dance at Willington the week after that. Attending dances was handy for us because it wasn't too expensive. Although Joan was earning her own money at Wilkinson, I wasn't exactly what you could call flush. You see, when I first got to the camp I was restricted to a shilling a day because there had been some sort of cock up while I was travelling around the world with the touring band. Apparently, I'd been paid as an adult all that time so I was told I would have to pay back the difference. Therefore when I arrived in Durham I was already in debt to the Army, so they restricted my pay until it was made up. All I was left with was seven bob a week, which didn't stretch all that far. To supplement my income, I did a bit of extra work around the camp, cleaning for the other fellas, pressing uniforms, polishing boots, that sort of thing. I'd already been in the Army for more than three years by now so I was used to it and, if I say so myself, pretty darned good at it. More often than not, Joan would insist on paying for nights out, which I simply hated. I didn't like her subsidizing me. I didn't think it was right. But she insisted on doing it nevertheless.

It wasn't long before the pair of us were officially courting, seeing each other as much as we could but always wary not to attract too much attention to ourselves as we were both worried what might happen if Joan's dad ever found out about us. It was real Romeo and Juliet stuff! She was convinced that he wouldn't be at all happy that one of his daughters was cavorting around the place with a young soldier. He'd been one himself – fighting in the First World War – he didn't want one of his daughters walking out with a 'here today, gone tomorrow' soldier.

To ensure we could see each other for longer on nights out, Joan would arrange to stay at her brother Henry's house near the camp, careful not to let on she was seeing a soldier. Henry was a lovely chap, almost 30 at the time and a fitter down the pit. If machinery needed repairing, Henry was your man. But, as lovely as he was, we didn't dare tell him about our courtship, just in case he let slip to their dad.

Sometimes, Henry's job at the pit meant he would have to work overnight during the week or at weekends. When Joan confided in Henry's wife, Joyce, about our blossoming relationship, they agreed that when Henry was away, she would stay over to keep Joyce company. In reality, Joan would turn up at the house with me in tow and, after a chat and a cup of hot tea, Joyce would very kindly retire to her room so that the pair of us could have some much-needed alone time.

Up until this point, our relationship had been pretty innocent, sneaking gentle pecks whenever we could. For one, we wanted to keep our relationship on the quiet, so that word never got back to Joan's family. But also, we weren't exactly a showy couple. We were modest and wanted to take our time. In the safety of Henry's house, Joan and I felt comfortable to be intimate, but always within reason – just a few snogs here and there, nothing too heavy.

Joan and I had talked about taking things further, but that's all it was – talk. It wasn't really for Joan at that time and I respected her wishes. Of course, I was young and eager, but I respected Joan and I was in no rush to become too intimate too fast. I had such strong feelings for Joan and genuinely believed that she would one day be my wife that I was quite happy to wait for that special moment.

It's funny, at 19, I hadn't experienced much romance in my life, not like the other lads I knew. In fact, it was pretty uneventful. I'd snuck the odd kiss from a girl at a dance from time to time, but there was never anyone who had really meant anything to me.

As the weeks drifted by, our courtship continued in a very tasteful way. If Joan was unable to stay over at Henry's, I would go out of my way to walk her up the steep hill back home to Oakenshaw, the small little mining village where she lived with her mam, dad and four of her six sisters. Her other two sisters had by then married and left home, along with her brother, Henry. By the time we made it up to the top, we'd both be exhausted and out of breath, which gave us the perfect opportunity to take a rest and enjoy each other's company for just a little while longer. Once recovered, I'd then walk her to her door and, as quietly as possible, give her a long and lingering kiss goodnight on the doorstep before dashing back down the hill to the camp.

This hiding-in-the-shadows routine carried on for several weeks with no one twigging – but it wasn't long before our secret was finally exposed.

CHAPTER 4

Meeting the family

'Oh Joan,' I sighed, as we strolled up the hill, hand in hand, towards her parents' house after another village dance, 'I don't think I have ever felt as happy as I do now.' Joan squeezed my hand and snuggled her head into my shoulder, giggling gently.

'Oh Hunk,' she chuckled, using one of the many nicknames she would give me over the years, 'I wish we could bottle this and make it last forever.'

Yes, when you're in love, you really do talk in clichés. And yet, as soppy as those words I said to Joan may have sounded, I meant every single one of them.

It had been yet another joyous night in the village. We'd danced ourselves silly and laughed ourselves hoarse and we'd kissed as if the world was about to end. We even talked about the future – our future – and I was pleased to hear that Joan wanted the same things as me. We talked about enjoying a life together, perhaps even getting married one day and the joy that having kids would bring us. I may have been just shy of 20 years old, but I was grown-up enough to know what I wanted. I wanted to throw myself into a relationship full of love and devotion, like the ones you read about in great romance novels or see in epic films such as *Gone With The Wind*. I wanted to have something my own parents didn't have – a happy, loving and respectful marriage. What I could remember about Mother and Father being together really wasn't worth thinking about. Their marriage was far from happy and all they appeared to do was argue and slam doors or storm out of the house and disappear for long spells of time. I never saw them happily together, never saw them embrace, never saw them even hold hands.

I think in some ways I had always been looking for that great love. Perhaps when you don't experience it yourself, you tend to search high and low for it. And in Joan I found it. From the very first moment I saw her at that dance, I was convinced she was the girl for me. Don't ask me why, but I was. It may, admittedly, have started out as infatuation, but sometimes infatuation turns into love. The more and more I got to know her, the more perfect she became. Similarly, Joan had come to the happy realization that perhaps I actually was the man for her. She had told me before that the reason she'd dashed off that first night was because she reckoned I was a bit of a Jack-the-lad who didn't take life seriously and had an eye for the ladies. However, she also confessed that she fancied me like mad, as she loved a man in uniform.

Arriving at her house, we said our usual goodnights to one another and I dashed off into the night. Once I'd disappeared safely from view, Joan proceeded into the house, popped her head into the living room to say goodnight to her parents before carrying on up to bed. However, her dad's voice stopped her suddenly in her tracks. 'Don't you think it's about time we saw this lad of yours?' he called out.

Joan froze on the spot. 'What lad?' she stammered.

'Why, that soldier lad you've been knocking around with,' her dad responded, without looking up from his paper.

Joan knew there was no point in arguing with her dad. It would appear that whispers had made it back to the village and he knew what was going on. She was cornered. She shuffled uneasily into the room to fight her case, her dad eyeing her coolly. 'You know what I think about soldier lads,' he said, raising his arm in the air to reveal the shiny hook that had replaced the hand he'd lost in the Battle of the Somme in 1916. 'They're no good, my dear girl. None of them.'

'But he is different,' she pleaded. 'Colin is a gentleman.'

Her dad raised an eyebrow. 'Ah, Colin, is it?'

'Yes,' she half whispered.

'What makes this soldier lad so different to others, eh?'

For what seemed an age, the pair sparred with each other, her dad sticking to his guns about the worthlessness of soldiers as suitors for his daughter. Meanwhile, Joan fought my corner, pleading with him to give me a chance before making any rash judgements. It must have worked, because somewhere during their war of words her dad took her by surprise, telling her to invite me for a Sunday lunch to meet the family.

When Joan informed me of the invitation, I couldn't believe my ears. Her strict, soldier-hating dad was actually willing to let me into the house. What a turn-up for the books!

I was overjoyed, though when the day finally arrived to meet the family, I was riddled with nerves. Although I was confident that I would win them over, I was aware that I would be judged by not just her dad, but also her mam and her numerous siblings.

In order to impress her folks, I slipped into my best military uniform, gave my shoes a thorough once-over and made sure I looked the part of the dutiful boyfriend. Then, heading out earlier than I needed to, I took a casual stroll up the hill so I didn't break out into a sticky sweat. It was important that I arrived looking spick and span, not a dribbling mess.

As I approached the house, I began to feel nervous again, which is rather strange when you consider I had been in the Army for so long and had little fear taking on the enemy. But this was different. Today I was coming face to face not with a foe, but with someone I was desperately trying to get on side.

I approached the door but before I made my presence known I cleared my throat, adjusted my jacket one last time and wiped away a light layer of sweat from my forehead. Then tap, tap, tap.

I could hear movement from within the house followed by the approaching shuffle of feet. The door opened slowly to reveal Joan's mam, Alice.

'Good afternoon,' I beamed, holding out a hand to greet her.

'Hello son,' she replied distractedly, 'come on through.'

She was an attractive woman with white hair, but there was something amiss, I could tell straightaway. It looked as if she had been crying. I followed her through to the sitting room, where a long table was immaculately laid out for what promised to be a sumptuous meal.

Around the table stood Joan, her dad Norman, her sisters Monica, Marie, Adele and Yvonne, and her brother Henry with his wife Joyce, all of whom looked rather upset.

I swallowed hard. What had I walked into? Was it something I had said or done without realizing?

I went to shake Norman's hand, but he raised a deadly looking hook. Ah yes, I'd forgotten about that, so I saluted him instead. Joan had previously explained how her dad, a former miner, had lost his arm during the Battle of the Somme back in the First World War. He had actually injured his arm earlier in the war and come home to have it treated. Once healed, he had gallantly returned to the front line, where he was injured a second time, only on this occasion medics were unable save his arm. Back home again, he was fitted with a false hand that he wore mainly for formal occasions but found so cumbersome that he preferred instead to wear his hook, which took many grown-ups by surprise but seemed to enchant kids no end. In fact, when Joan and I had our kids later in life, they loved their grandfather's hook so much and would hold on to it every time they went out together. Interestingly, when he attached his prosthetic hand, they would never hold it. But the hook? They simply couldn't get enough of that sharp, shiny appendage. It was normal to them. He was Grandad, and Grandad didn't have two hands. Simple.

Norman's injuries meant that he was no longer able to work down the mines but, after the war, his employers were duty-bound to give him a job and enrolled him on a book-keeping course before offering him a job in the cabin at the top of the pit, where he would record everything. To supplement his income, Norman took a second job as the steward of the local Conservative Club in the village. There, he would sing and dance, and rope in his daughters to perform a clog dance with him at parties. I was pleased to hear the family shared my love of music and dancing.

Joan dashed to my side and grabbed my arm. She, too, looked visibly upset.

'What's going on? What's happened?' I asked, panicking, my eyes darting from one family member to the next.

Joan started to sob and pressed her head against my chest.

Alice stepped forward and explained that their dear family dog, a handsome spaniel whose name I can't for the life of me remember, had passed. As the words came out of her mouth, I could see the family all sob in unison. I swear I even saw stoic Norman use his good hand to discreetly wipe what was quite possibly a tear from his eye.

Alice squeezed my arm and said to me quietly. 'You wouldn't do us the greatest favour and help bury our beloved dog?'

What a day this was turning out to be. Here I was coming to meet the family for a wholesome Sunday lunch and now I was being asked to be undertaker for their deceased dog. It felt as though I was being put to the test and closely observed to see if I was worthy enough for their daughter.

'Of course,' I replied, feeling cornered. 'But do you have a change of clothes I could wear? I'm wearing my best uniform and don't want to get it dirty.'

'Of course,' Alice replied. 'Let me fetch you something.'

Slipping into some overalls and a pair of wellies, I followed Norman into another room where their deceased pooch lay. It was a beautiful animal, more beautiful no doubt when it had been breathing, and I could understand why the family were so upset. I told Norman to return to the others while I rolled the canine into a rug, thinking it best that he not see the lifeless hound being so unceremoniously disposed of.

Norman returned with a shovel and led us down the yard, across the street and into the allotments that were opposite. When we found a spot that seemed discreet enough for a burial, Norman advised I 'dig the hole deep', which I did. Again, as I plunged the shovel into the ground, I couldn't help wonder if Norman was watching my every move as a way of working out whether or not I was good enough for his daughter.

Whether that was really the case or not, it seemed to have done the trick because when I returned to the house, I was treated like the hero of the hour, even by hard-to-please Norman, who I think was impressed by my gallant work. It certainly wasn't how I had imagined the day playing out. Looking back, it was quite the introduction to the family.

After a quick wash, I slipped back into my uniform and joined the family in the living room for lunch. Alice was very grateful and gave me a peck on the cheek and insisted that from now on I call her 'mum' or 'mam', as those up north tended to say. As my relationship with my own mother was fractured, I was happy to call this warm-hearted woman 'mam'.

The table, as I said, was beautifully laid out with table mats and cutlery all in place. Alice insisted Henry, Norman and I take our seats while she and the girls busied themselves preparing dishes in the kitchen. The rule of the house in these times was that the men would always be seated at the table while the women tended to the catering. As I breathed in the delicious aromas emanating from the kitchen, Norman and I chatted about my time in the Army and where I'd grown up. I had been expecting some kind of interrogation, but was surprised to find that Norman's line of questioning was anything but. In fact, he was gentle, inquisitive and appeared to be genuinely interested in finding out who I was, just as I was of him. He explained that they didn't see too many Londoners around their parts and was fascinated to see if I was one of those 'huggy' and 'kissy' Londoner types. The family also considered me to be posh, which amused me no end, bearing in mind the rough-and-ready upbringing I'd experienced on the poor streets of Camden. In fact, for many years, two of Joan's sisters constantly referred to me as a posh boy!

Our conversation was halted suddenly when Joan glided into the room with a waft of cooking smells, carrying what looked like a huge Yorkshire pudding on a dish and placed it in front of me, warning me not to burn my fingers on the edge of the plate. It was a strange, oblong shape that was roughly eight inches by four. I'd never seen anything like it. It really was quite extraordinary.

'What a spectacle,' I laughed, not quite sure what to make of this massive beast laid before me. I assumed that as 'guest of honour' I would be required to cut it up and pass it around to everyone else. But as I started to mentally count up how many servings would be needed, I noticed everyone's eyes were fixed on me.

'What are you doing with that?' Alice asked quizzically.

'I'm cutting it up so everyone can have a slice,' I replied.

'Don't you like Yorkshire pudding?' she said with an accusatory tone in her voice.

'I do,' I replied, licking my lips. 'I love it.'

'Well, get it down you, lad,' she laughed, 'because that's yours.'

I laughed again, thinking she was pulling my leg. I swear to you, the Yorkshire pud could quite easily have fed the whole family and the family next door to boot. I was later informed that in the local area you traditionally start your lunch with an obscenely large Yorkshire pudding as a belly filler, which this certainly was.

Always up for a challenge, I took a deep breath and dug in. I wasn't disappointed. The Yorkshire pudding was absolutely delicious, even more so when I drenched it in steaming hot gravy.

The main event was roast beef with all the trimmings and every bite was a treat. There was one particular ingredient that was a mystery to me, which I guessed must be another local delight. It was an orangey-red-looking mash that tasted absolutely delicious. And, as I savoured it in my mouth, I couldn't for the life of me identify it.

'It's turnip,' Joan informed me, looking astonished at my supposed ignorance. 'Mashed turnip.'

'But turnip's white,' I replied. It turns out that up north they called swede turnip. That was the first time I'd had a mashed swede, but certainly not the last. I had previously only ever had it chopped up into bits and thrown into a stew.

Throughout the meal I noticed that Alice paid close attention to me and looked almost gleeful every time I took a mouthful of food. Even before I'd cleaned my plate, she'd push one of the vegetable dishes towards me and encourage me to have some more. As a lover of good food, I didn't hesitate in saying 'yes'. I loved my food and I had been taught in the Army never to leave anything behind, so if it was offered, you were supposed to accept it, to enjoy it and to feel free to ask for more afterwards.

Alice, it turned out, was of a similar persuasion. After the meal she confided in me that she had found great pleasure in watching me eat. 'I am fed up of cooking for fussy eaters like my daughters,' she scolded. 'They just pick at food, like girls tend to.'

When lunch was over and we had enjoyed tea and pudding, I reluctantly said my goodbyes to Joan and the family, and headed back to camp with a spring in my step and warmth in my heart. It was still early days, but I was now totally convinced that I had found the woman I would spend the rest of my life with. And what made things better was that her family appeared to accept me and love me as if I were their own.

As I replayed scenes from earlier in the day through my mind, it wasn't lost on me that this new life I was beginning to lead was a far cry from the tough and lonely existence I had endured growing up on the streets of dirty pre-war London, not knowing where Mother or Father were half the time and never really getting to know my brothers or sisters until later on in life.

PART 2

1930s London

CHAPTER 5

A scamp on the streets

When I was a young kid, I never realised that my family was as dysfunctional as it was, but then I had nothing to compare it to. It was only many years later, when I met my in-laws, that I finally understood what being part of a family actually meant.

Don't get me wrong, Mother and Father weren't exactly bad parents. We had a roof over our heads and food on the table. But that was it. No money, no toys and sometimes no interest in what I did.

In retrospect, I think they were so caught up in their own unhappiness that they really didn't know how to look after children and so didn't notice if I was actually there or not. Of course, at the time, I was oblivious to everything that was going on around me. All I knew was that parents argued a lot and sometimes mothers would disappear for days on end. That was just the way it was.

But I didn't mind, as that gave me the freedom to do whatever I wanted. When I was old enough to walk and know my way around, I would go out at the crack of dawn and stay out until dusk, and nobody noticed. And that's the way I liked it – coming and going when I pleased, no one to tell me to do anything, no one to force me to go to school. I didn't, of course. Instead, I lived on the streets of filthy, squalid Camden Town, finding amusement wherever

I could and nicking stuff from the shops with the other kids who lived around the area.

I was way too young then to know what was going on with Mother and Father but, in subsequent years, I have grown to understand why things might have been so very difficult for them.

When Albert Thackery saw the pretty waitress darting across the room delivering tea, it was love at first sight. She was a petite brunette and had the prettiest face he had ever seen. Of course, when dining at the well-known establishment, Lyons' Corner House, you expected to see only the most beautiful girls tending tables. The waitresses were popularly known as 'Nippies' and were always clad in maid-like outfits with matching hats. During the 1920s, they had become something of a national institution after appearing in various advertising campaigns, so everyone in the country knew what a Nippy was. Because they had become such iconic figures, their bosses insisted that only the prettiest girls be employed as Nippies, no doubt as a ruse to get more gentlemen to frequent the tea house and spend big. Albert, a drummer with the Royal Scots and now working as a porter at a chocolate factory, while also being a part-time soldier in the Territorial Army, might not have been a big spender, but he certainly enjoyed what he saw. Waving over the pretty brunette to take his order, he flashed her a killer smile that made her blush, asked her name and made it clear that he was interested in more than just a cup of piping hot tea.

A few weeks later the pretty Nippy, Lilian Jacobs, discovered she was pregnant and her life changed beyond all recognition. She was just 15 years old.

Lilian was the daughter of renowned boxer and boxing promoter, Harry Jacobs. Everyone in the boxing fraternity knew who he was and they had the utmost respect for him. Reputation meant everything to him, so if he was hit by any scandal, he would do anything to ensure it got sorted.

For many years my family were under the impression that when Harry found out that his youngest daughter had not only fallen pregnant at the tender age of 15, but had fallen pregnant to a man who wasn't Jewish, he went ballistic. It was believed that he demanded of Lilian that when she gave birth to me, she would hand me over to him so that he could bring me up himself. In return for not being kicked out of home, she would then have to promise never to see my father again. In spite of her youthful years, legend has it that Mother declined her father's generous offer, telling him she wanted to stick with Albert. Unsurprisingly, her father let rip and disowned her there and then.

Well, that's what I grew up believing, anyway. Recently, research into our family tree suggests that this story may not actually be true after all. It now emerges that Harry died on 6 February 1929 – over a year before I was born on 9 March 1930, which means he actually died before Lilian even fell pregnant. In light of this, we now think that it may have been one of her uncles, who took on all of his brother's business interests after his death, who banished Lilian from the family for bringing shame on the Jacobs household.

Whatever the situation, it is understood that when Lilian married Albert Thackery on 21 July 1929, she never spoke to any of her family again.

Married life wasn't a walk in the park for Albert, either. His doting parents, Elizabeth and Thomas Thackery, made it clear that they were not happy about him marrying a Jewish girl and they also decided to have absolutely no relationship or communication with his young bride whatsoever. So began a relationship that would be full of unhappiness and ultimately doomed.

Even when I was very young, I was aware that Mother and Father's marriage was not a happy one. They bickered incessantly, screaming at each other about the little things, and never really showed each other much affection.

In fairness to my mother, looking back at the situation with fresh eyes, circumstances weren't the easiest for her. Father was much older than she was – at least ten years older – so I assume that it must have dawned on them soon after they were married that they had very little in common.

It also probably didn't help that my father's side of the family despised her so much. I only knew this because my Nan – to whom I would be sent during their 'break-ups' and who loved me greatly – would never speak of 'that woman' and, if she had to, it certainly wasn't in a kind way. For one, I got the impression that my Nan thought my mother had trapped her golden boy by getting herself pregnant, potentially ruining any fruitful future he may have carved out for himself. Secondly, I think Nan hated her because Mother was Jewish. Back then, the Jews had a difficult life and were physically and verbally abused on the street by people every day. Jewish people had a really hard time of it, and I fear my mother may have fallen victim to that. I can imagine that she must have felt very isolated and lonely, and I think this contributed to a marriage fraught with difficulties.

In spite of my parents' woes, I think I loved my mother, even if sometimes she was distracted and did not always show me affection. She was an easy-going kind of girl, not difficult to get on well with, but that's really all I can remember. People tend to blot out the unhappy moments in one's life and only recall the good things. In truth, I'm talking about someone of whom I didn't see all that much of, and when I did, it was when she and Father were going at it hammer and tongs.

In my eyes, Father was a great man, but I remember that he had one hell of a temper, although luckily he never took it out on me. I guess his fiery temper is why he had been nicknamed 'Tiger'. He was a short man at 5ft 3in, but he made up for it with a big personality. During the 1920s, he had been a regular soldier with the Royal Scots and had been posted overseas in various places including India, where he had been a flyweight boxer. A good one at that!

When I was about seven, Father became the Bugle Major of the London Irish Rifles, a Territorial battalion stationed at the Duke of York Barracks in Chelsea. He played the drums and would practise at home all the time. He encouraged me to practise with him, which I loved doing and took to very well. Sometimes his constant tapping would drive Mother mad and she would have a go at him, so eventually he stopped doing it and practised instead on softer furnishings.

From what I remember he was always in uniform, which included a busby hat. A green plume would poke out of the front of it because it was an Irish regiment. He also wore a cross belt with whistles carried inside. Father had to have his stick and sword shortened because he was so short – otherwise they'd have dragged along the floor. I would go along to watch him with total pride. It was so exhilarating to see him and all the soldiers marching. I guess it must have put the idea of becoming a soldier into my head. Mother never came along to see him.

For a while, it was just the three of us – Mother, Father and me, all living in a tenement house on Bayham Street in Camden Town. It was a very shabby, rundown house with just two bedrooms and small enough to hear every spoken word or raised voice. After their stormy rows, Mother and Father would separate for a while and then get back together again, and before you knew it, there'd be another baby on the way. This means they must have broken up and reunited at least five times, as they went on to have five other children: Shirley, Michael, Maisie, John (who died in childhood of an unknown illness) and Brian, who was only a baby at the time of the final split. Having so many kids in one house was hard, though, because there wasn't much room. Mother and Father would take the youngest in with them to start with and then, when another came along, they would be replaced and sent to join me and the others in what was originally my room. It did get a little bit overcrowded – sometimes we'd all be squeezed into the same bed – so I tried to stay out of the house as much as I could.

The family, as I said, had little money, but we always had food on the table. My parents never bought me toys, so when I'd roam the streets with the local kids, we'd either end up pinching toys from the local Woolies or we'd make our own. We would hunt for bits of wood and use it to make scooters with ball-bearing wheels, scrounged from garages or wherever we could find them. If you were really clever, you could even make a sidecar. Looking back, they were quite sophisticated contraptions for children of our age, but they made an almighty racket as we went careering up and down the streets and we were always getting chased off by someone or other who didn't like the noise.

Of course, we never went on holiday. I think the closest I ever got to going anywhere was when my Aunty Maisie – Father's sister – took me to Southend for the day, which I loved because I had never seen the sea before. It was utterly enthralling – completely different to the time Mother decided to take us hop picking in Kent. This was something that a lot of poor families did every year. The harvesting of hops, used to brew beer, was so highly labour-intensive that farmers needed lots of workers to help out, so they would ship in families from poor areas of the country and pay them a small amount of money for doing the work.

Farmers would send out hop cards to people's homes, each one allocating a place for a family on a particular hop farm. It was an opportunity that was very popular with folk. In fact, so many people wanted to get their hands on those cards that a black market developed in stolen and forged cards.

For many families, this journey to the countryside was the closest they'd ever get to having a holiday. Special trains were laid on from London Bridge to transport families to the hop fields in Kent. Some families couldn't afford the train ticket but were desperate to earn a bit of money so they would walk for miles to the hop gardens at Paddock Wood, Maidstone and Faversham, sleeping by the roadside when they got tired.

Conditions at the hop farms were pretty basic. We stayed in unheated sheds and slept on straw-stuffed mattresses piled on twigs. It was awful. We cooked over fires outdoors or in huge concrete cookhouses and washed our clothes in local streams. While the farmers might give us a bit of fruit to eat, we'd have to save up money for meat. The people who lived in the area viewed us all with suspicion. Pub landlords would worry about having their tankards stolen by the hoppers so would serve them drinks in jam jars. Meanwhile, us kids were banned from village shops because we were apparently riddled with fleas!

Sometimes the Salvation Army would come along and hand out milk and cakes for us kids, while the British Red Cross offered us cups of Oxo and a board game for a penny. A family could earn up to around £40 for the hop-picking season if they were lucky – that was a lot of money for some people. Work would start at seven or eight in the morning and hoppers would carry on picking until about lunchtime. After lunch, they'd carry on until five. While Mother earned some money from our time in Kent, I found it to be a depressing experience, living in a cold hut with no electricity or water. I couldn't wait to get back to dirty, grubby Camden, thank you very much. At least it was home!

When I lived with Mother and Father, I was signed up for school but I very rarely attended. The only time I did go was when I was staying with my paternal grandmother and my aunt, just up the road, and that's because they made me go. I can't remember for the life of me what the school was called or where it was, but I would occasionally go for the morning and then end up gallivanting around the area like an urchin for the rest of the day.

On the rare occasion I did attend school, I enjoyed spelling – because I was good at it – and I loved playing the triangle or tambourine in the school band. I wasn't much good at anything else. I found sums quite hard, so I would end up getting bored and messing around in class instead. If I'm honest, I wasn't in school long enough to learn properly – looking back, I regret that a lot. When I went to Boys' Service at 15, I discovered that I had a school age of just 9, so I was way behind. In those days, you could miss classes and nothing would get said. No teachers, as far as I know, ever got in touch with my parents about my bad behaviour. No one seemed to care. My parents were well aware that I was skipping school, but they never said anything to me. Mother and Father weren't exactly the strictest of parents, though it would have been good if they had had been. Sometimes the police would catch me cutting school and march me back there – but then I'd slip back out again.

I wasn't the only scamp, of course. There were loads of kids running riot on the streets and causing havoc. Although I hung around with a bunch of boys from the area, I wouldn't describe them as friends. We never shared secrets, never confided in each other and I can't remember any of their names or what they looked like. We were just a bunch of kids who had nothing to do, who were bonded by boredom and who got chased a lot by the police.

If my memory serves me correctly, we kept the coppers pretty busy chasing after us all the time, but we'd always manage to outsmart and/or outrun them because we were so nimble. We may have been little but, boy, we could move. We were wily, too, and headed for the places we knew the coppers couldn't fit through, slipping through the railings leaving a fiery sergeant standing there looking exasperated.

CHAPTER 6

Causing a kerfuffle

As you can tell, I was a right little tearaway when I was a kid, one of those wily little devils who was always up to no good and on the prowl for mischief or a way of making a few bob. Even though I had Mother and Father and a roof over my head, I was at my happiest running around the streets of Camden, bunking off school, nicking a bread roll off a passing bakery cart or outrunning the coppers who'd caught me and my mates getting up to no good.

This was what life was like for most of us kids in post-Depression London. Poverty was rife, prospects were non-existent and so, while mums and dads were out working trying to make ends meet, us kids were left to our own devices, running around the filthy streets in raggedy socks, covered head to toe in muck and with absolutely no desire to go home.

It's not that home was an awful place, I'd be lying if I said it was. There was always some kind of food on the table and sometimes Mother and Father wouldn't be screaming at each other, which made for a pleasant change. But home was boring, there was nothing to do. There were no toys to speak of and only families with money had a wireless, so what kid in their right mind would want to stay home in a smelly room, when they could be making their own fun with a bunch of kids on the streets.

And that fun came in various forms. Sometimes me and some of the lads would head down to the local Woolworths on a mission to get our sticky paws on toy soldiers, sweets or anything that caught our eye. We did it so often that we were able to refine our skills to the point that the security men or cashiers wouldn't know anything was going on. We dreamed up inventive ways of causing a distraction for the shop's employees. While one or two of us would be set a mission to cause a kerfuffle near the staff member, our other lads would leg it down the aisles and grab whatever they could, while a 'watchman' would keep a beady eye on security. Most of the time, we'd get away scot-free, without anyone ever noticing. But the more we did it, the more savvy the Woolworths' staff became, which meant sometimes they would twig what we were up to and would be ready and waiting for our next attack.

We had a lot of madcap schemes that kept us entertained. Some mornings, we'd sneak out of bed early to hijack the horse-led bakery carts that would rattle down the streets of Camden delivering a fresh batch of tasty-smelling bread rolls to the local cafés, grocers and hotels. Our initial attacks were quite spontaneous, as we never knew when a delivery would be winding its way along the streets, or from which direction. However, after a few mornings, we started to notice patterns, which made it easier for us to plan properly. We'd all gather at a certain time of a morning, come up with a plan of action and lie in wait, just like Dick Turpin or some other cunning highwayman. Normally, a couple of the front-line guys would hop up onto the back of the cart and gather as many buns as they could before firing them over to the support party, who would bag them up and dash off before the driver was any the wiser. Once the driver had worked out he was under attack, he'd jump off his cart and chase the front-line boys down the street, waving his whip above his head. Of course, we were very much aware that if we wanted this system to work more than once, we would have to keep our raids as varied and spontaneous as possible by targeting various drivers on different routes so that they were always taken by surprise.

Although what we were doing was basically stealing, I couldn't help but be a little proud of our ingenuity and business sense. Everywhere we went, the lads and I always kept a keen eye out for any opportunities that could make us a few bob. At this particular time, trams were being phased out of service, so workmen around London had started pulling up tram tracks and the wooden blocks they were encased in. Somehow, we discovered that this wood was soaked in tar and oil, which meant that it would burn beautifully – we thought it might prove to be a bit of a money-maker. You see, one thing we knew people wanted to get their hands on at all times was wood for their fireplaces and they were willing to pay a halfpenny for it. To get the wood, we had to pull it up from the ground, but this wasn't easy as a nightwatchman kept an eye on the site from his cabin, so we used our old two-party distraction trick. One of us would chat to him while the rest of us would sneak over to where the wooden blocks were and, as quietly and as fast as we could, chip away at them until they came loose. Then we'd throw them into a cart that we'd made for the enterprise, dash off and flog them to people for a halfpenny or sometimes even a penny. Everyone knew they were pinched, but that's the way it was back then.

We weren't always nicking stuff. Sometimes, for a lark, we'd go to London Zoo to have a look at the animals. I loved seeing animals up close, especially the giraffes and elephants. They were unlike anything you'd see anywhere else. Of course, we'd never pay to get in – it cost a fortune – but us crafty lads had stumbled upon a way of sneaking in without anyone knowing. We had previously found a way to get across a certain part of Regent's Canal, by jumping on an iron fence, swinging back and forth on it to work up enough momentum to launch ourselves over to the other side of the Canal and into the Zoo. Sometimes it worked, other times it didn't and we'd plunge into the filthy canal water and laugh like hyenas. But on the occasions we did make it across, we'd dash around the Zoo, trying to take in as many of the animals as we could. This was such a contrast to our everyday world, and to see animals from the wild was simply extraordinary. Although we were total scamps, we treated the animals with respect and never tried to upset them in any way. One of my favourite animals that I would always see without fail was the famous London Zoo gorilla. He was absolutely huge and, to a little eight-year-old boy like me, he looked just like King Kong, which I found both scary and fascinating all at once. Sometimes, while the other lads dashed around to look at the other animals, I would just stare at this massive primate, totally mesmerized by him.

The picture house was another of our favourite hangouts. Cowboy films were my favourite. In fact, for a time, I wanted to grow up to be a cowboy, until I realised that wasn't going to happen. Of course, strapped for cash as we constantly were, we tried every which way to get into the pictures without having to spend a penny. Our favourite method was getting one of the lads to buy a ticket for one of the screenings. Once he was in, he'd sneak to the back doors, which had those push-down handles, and let us in as quickly as possible before the ushers saw what we were up to. I loved watching films. It was an amazing escape from the grim reality we lived in, even if it was for just an hour or so. After the film, we'd be so full of energy and excitement that we'd bounce out of the picture house and 'pow, pow, pow', all the way along the street.

When I realised it was unlikely that I'd end up a cowboy, I decided I wanted to be a G-Men Detective instead. He was the star of a relatively new American comic strip. Not only would he go on exciting missions, but he also had this amazing wrist radio, with which he could speak to headquarters. In those days, the idea of a wristwatch that you could use to communicate with people simply blew all our young minds and, of course, we wanted to have one. So we did what kids with no money do and improvized, by wrapping a bunch of elastic bands around our wrists and speaking into them.

It was hard to dream about a future, growing up in such a poor area. Yes, some of us spoke about wanting to be doctors or lawyers, but we knew that it was very unlikely that we'd ever get the chance to fulfil our dreams. Even at that this early stage, I did toy with the idea of becoming a soldier. I mean, it felt like the next best thing after being a cowboy. My father was in the Army, so that may have sparked my interest. I also rather enjoyed the fact that soldiers got to lead adventurous lives, become heroes and get to wear a uniform. I loved the idea of wearing a uniform, which is why I also thought of becoming a policeman.

Despite the petty villainy, we had respect for figures of authority and we held them in high regard. We were wary of coppers and most grown-ups were very strict with us. I remember standing on the roadside once, just as a funeral procession went by, and someone whipped my hat off my head and snapped, 'Where's your respect, you little bugger?' Discipline has always been a big thing in my mind and that has stayed with me. I always respected doctors and teachers; the policemen might scare you, but they were okay.

When I became a teenager, I decided it might be a good idea to stop nicking stuff and actually get out there and make some money of my own. For a while I worked as a delivery boy for a posh grocery shop called Fenns, delivering purchases to the big houses in Regent's Park. When I strolled past those palatial buildings, I thought three things: one, what do they look like inside? Two, what kind of person lives there? And three, will I ever earn enough money to buy a place like that? Three things I have yet to discover. Back then, those big houses were a bit like Downton Abbey, where the posh people lived upstairs and the cooks, butlers and all the servants were below stairs. I used to get on with the cooks and would sit at their table and have tea and cake and a good gas.

Despite my lack of interest in school, when it came to working at Fenns, I was really quite committed and I learned a lot there. It was a very high-end shop. Downstairs, all the game was prepared for the table. The old boy in charge showed me how to skin rabbits, defeather birds, and how to prepare them for the table.

I also earned a few bob helping out a local greengrocer. It was a tiring job, though – I would have to get up at an ungodly hour to go to Covent Garden to help my boss carry heavy sacks of spuds around. Even though I was still only 12, I was quite stocky – strong and built like a little man.

It wasn't just boys in the gang that I hung around in. There were the odd girls too, but they were mainly tomboys. To be honest, girls weren't particularly welcome, as is often the case with boys when they are young. It was different when we got a bit older and then we'd nip down an alleyway and sneak a kiss. But that's all there was to it. It was very innocent, back then, we were very chaste and you'd be lucky to get a kiss. None of us knew very much – when I was about 9, I remember learning from a boy of 16 about how babies were produced and I thought it was disgusting. I went home and said to my parents, 'How dare you – what you did was awful!' I really couldn't believe that parents would do that sort of thing.

CHAPTER 7

Refuge with my grandparents

Whenever Mother and Father argued or one of them left the house, I would automatically be sent off to stay with my paternal grandparents, Thomas and Elizabeth Thackery. Not that I minded in the slightest as I loved them dearly. They lived in a very ordinary terraced house just between Mornington Crescent and Tottenham Court Road. Oddly, my siblings never came with me – I have no idea why. Perhaps my mother was more interested in the other kids because they were younger and she wanted to keep them close by. But Nan always sniped that Mother was only interested in having babies because as they grew older, she seemed less interested in them.

Nan was very proud of her home and she kept it looking very spick and span. She was extremely fussy about washing and ironing. She had an old-fashioned iron, which she heated on the fire. You weren't allowed to wear anything unless it had been washed, ironed and aired. They didn't have a garden, but they had a back yard where stray cats would roam. She hated them and would dash outside to chase them away, carrying her corsets in her hand. It was an extraordinary sight and is a vivid memory for me, even today.

Nan was a small lady, an Irish Catholic. She was a men's tailor and a very skilled needlewoman. When I joined the Army, she had me go and get the biggest uniform I could find so that she could strip it completely and make it to measure. Even though she didn't like my mother, she once told me that she would only work for Jewish people because, she said, they were good payers.

She was efficient and a hard worker and her employers were very fond of her. When she was forced to take time off work due to her bronchial asthma, her boss would come round to see if she was doing okay and to make sure she had enough money.

Nan and Grandad fought like cat and dog, but not in the same way as Mother and Father. You could tell that my grandparents were very in love. Nan had a temper, but that was the Irish in her. Grandad was very mild until she had a go at him. She could be ferocious sometimes and it was a sight to see. She was in charge, no doubt about it.

Even though I was a bit of a tearaway, I was very well behaved with my grandparents and Nan never told me off too much. She had certain rules in the house. Firstly, you couldn't leave the table until you'd eaten everything. That was the way she had been brought up. She always insisted that we cleared our plates before excusing ourselves from the table. I never had any problems doing that. Even now I don't like to leave food. The other rule was not speaking while you were eating. She used to say, every time you speak you lose a mouthful. What on earth does that mean? It would take years before I started a conversation at a table. I used to find it very difficult to do that.

Every time Mother would banish me from the house while she did whatever it was she did, Nan would unpack everything I had, mend it and wash it. That was Nan. Nothing was right until she had administered to it. She also taught me to darn my own socks, which came in handy when I joined the Army.

I would help Nan out at home and take her washing to a place called a bag wash – basically like a launderette. It was run by a very handsome woman who rode a motorbike. She was unlike anyone I had ever seen – a very posh woman with black hair slicked back off her face. She wore skirts that had braces on them, which she would click to her boots, so that when she climbed upon the bike she retained her modesty.

Nan's daughter Maisie, my father's sister, was also very fond of me and treated me more like a son than my own mother did. In fact, there was a point where she actually wanted to adopt me, but Father refused. Like Nan, she absolutely adored Father and hated Mother, even though, years before, the pair of them had actually been very good friends. It was only when Mother fell pregnant with me and married my father that their friendship faltered. I think it might have been a case of it being fine to be friends with a Jewish girl, but to have one actually in the family was a very different kettle of fish.

Aunty Maisie, like all the family, was a small, round lady, full of fun. She continued to be fun all the way though her life. She never had kids of her own, which is a shame, and so saw me as the next best thing and would do anything for me. In fact, she thought the sun shone out of me. She'd buy me gifts, take me to places I had only dreamed about, like the seaside. She and her hilarious friend,

Dolly – who was married to a racing car mechanic – took me to Southend. It was the first time I had ever been to the beach and what an eye-opener that was. I was mesmerized by the tumbling waves – I had never seen anything like them – and to look out at the great expanse of sea made me wonder what lay beyond. Something I'd find out when I went to war in Korea.

Unlike Mother, Aunty Maisie was always buying me clothes. I think Maisie and Nan were appalled by how few clothes I had when I came to visit and they spoiled me rotten whenever they could. I guess I was a very lucky lad to have these wonderful women think so highly of me. It wasn't that Maisie had more money, but she was married and, with their combined wage, she was able to splash out a bit more than my parents could. Her first husband was Mr Patience, a foreman at a wood yard. Later, she married a chap called Jack Doherty and she became Mrs Doherty.

Auntie Dolly, as I came to call her, was eccentric and she would often be seen speeding around in a sports car wearing a very stylish floppy hat. It wasn't her car, of course. I think her husband, who was always in the driving seat, may have occasionally borrowed a car he was working on. Dolly always sang her husband's praises, telling me how wonderful he was at fixing cars and motorcycles. He loved his job so much that he'd literally bring it home and sometimes Dolly would walk into her kitchen to find a motorbike in bits all over the floor. One of his favourite phrases that he used to describe the service his company offered was, 'Door to door service, delivered to you straight to the door'. And it was true. When he delivered the car back to the customer, he would drive it right up to the front door. He was an absolutely crazy guy and sometimes he would drive me round in one of the sports cars he'd be working on, whizzing around the streets like we were in a racing competition. I felt so posh as we tore through the streets – no one had cars like that round our way, only rich people did, so just to be able to ride in a fancy sports car was amazing.

Every Saturday, Nan and Grandad would go to the local pub for their weekly night out and, if I was staying with them, they'd take me along too. Of course, I wasn't allowed inside, but they'd leave me on the steps outside and bring me out a bag of crisps and soft drinks.

This was their big night out and normally Grandad would end up getting up and singing a few songs. He was a very small man and I don't know where this voice came from, but it was enormously powerful – you could hear him a mile off. Often, I would hear people yelling, 'Come on Tom, sing us a song' and then he'd launch into a series of old musical classics, such as 'Any Old Iron'. The next thing you know, everyone's joining in – it was like a big old knees-up.

Although Nan and I were close, I also had a great relationship with Grandad. One of my most cherished memories from my childhood was going out with him on the horse and cart he had for work. He was a foreman driver for a firm that delivered corn, hay and oats to people who had horses. His horse, Nobby, was a sight to behold. It was a Percheron horse, a breed of carthorse that originated in the Huisne river valley in western France, and it was simply enormous. Usually grey or black in colour, Percherons are well muscled and known for their intelligence and willingness to work, and Nobby ticked every box. He was a beaut, and Grandad loved him like a child.

Whenever I went to stay with my grandparents, I would go to work with Grandad of a morning. We'd get up at God knows what hour, head to the stable and get Nobby prepared for the day, which always seemed to take an age. I'd lie across Nobby's neck and watch Grandad cleaning his tack. He was very fussy about the tack he used. He had a special cart and a special set of tack that only Grandad could touch, no one else was allowed to. I sensed that everyone who worked with him really respected and looked up to Grandad – even though he was so small!

After he'd set up the equipment, he'd walk us swiftly to where we could stock up on supplies to take to the firm's customers that morning. With his pipe in his mouth, he would storm ahead and, despite his short legs, I found it quite hard to keep up with him and I would be sweating within seconds.

Grandad Tom – Thomas Thackery – was a real London character. On our journey we would stop off at these coffee stalls and devour doorsteps of bread and dripping or bacon sandwiches, washed down with hot, strong tea with lots of sugar in it to give us energy for the day. He was a tough man, for sure, and I could tell that he wasn't frightened of anyone. Strangely, he had never been a soldier, though he had dug graves during the First World War.

Grandad and I had some really fun times with Nobby. I remember one hot, sunny day, Grandad drove us into a pond, with us still sitting in the cart. Just before doing that, he had stopped Nobby and put his nosebag on, and then he led him into the water. There we sat for a while, eating sandwiches and drinking cold tea from a bottle. Flasks were too posh for our kind! Then, when Grandad made a certain sound, Nobby pulled us out of the pond, we took his nosebag off and off we went again!

On the way back to the stables, we had to drive down a steep, winding cobbled road that was awkward to navigate. Grandad was always wary of this road because if a horse slipped, it could cause it a lot of damage and carts didn't have brakes to slow them down. Grandad added some chains to the wheels and made sure he drove the cart so the nearside wheel would scrape along the kerb to slow them down. That usually did the trick and Nobby would end up back at the stables, safe and well.

However, one day Grandad was too poorly to work and another driver took Nobby out on a job. Unlike Grandad, this fool didn't take the same care travelling down the cobbled hill and, as a result, Nobby fell. He was so badly injured that they had to pull him into a horse ambulance. After he was examined by the vet, it emerged that he had a strangulated hernia or something like that anyway. When Grandad heard what had happened, he hit the roof! He jumped out of his sick bed and headed straight for the stables, staying there for a month and nursing Nobby. Because Nobby was unable to pass his stools, Grandad would put his hand up Nobby's backside and help him with that. That's how much he loved that horse! However, he didn't show the driver as much love. In fact, he showed him no love at all and gave him a good beating with his whip.

Sadly, Nobby eventually died from his injuries, with Grandad by his side. Grandad was devastated by the loss, as was I. I had never seen Grandad cry before. It really hit him hard. Nobby's death also meant the end of one of Grandad's favourite pastimes. Every year he would enter his four-legged friend into the London Van Horse parade that took place at Easter in Regent's Park. Drivers would decorate their horses and carts and parade them around a circuit under the watchful gaze of a set of judges, who would appraise their style and elegance. Think Miss World, only with horses!

The reason Nobby's death hit Grandad so hard is because they had won the event together so many times and he knew exactly what it would take to win. The judges were looking out for signs of elegance and incredible presentation; all the special tack and cart had to look amazing – beautifully decorated, polished to perfection – and Grandad would never disappoint. The cart that Grandad used was only for funerals and competitions, and it looked stunning. The brass on the wheels and the cart was always polished until it shone like a twinkling star. Nobby would be spruced up for the day too – Grandad could never brush him down enough. Clever as she was with her hands, Nan would make ribbons that were plaited through Nobby's tail and she would place ribbon bows on his neck. Grandad would be decked out in his best suit with a bowler hat, and he always wore a buttonhole and a shirt and tie, tailored by Nan. Because he had the respect of so many of his peers, the other drivers would come out with their brushes and their polishing rags to help him make the cart look as good as it could.

Grandad and the other entrants would then be asked to drive round and round Regent's Park, during which time they would be scrutinized. The judges would then take a closer look at the horses' teeth and lift their feet to check whether their shoes were in good condition. It was a thorough inspection as it was a fierce competition, but Grandad was the king of this parade and would win rosettes every year.

After Nobby's death, Grandad had to get himself another horse for work. She was called Beth, but she was certainly no Nobby. She was only half broken, but Grandad could handle her. She had a trick of going off when she felt his foot on the shaft, so he would shout and then she would stop – but she would only obey him. It was amazing to watch.

Stupidly, one summer's day, I tried to show off to some of the local kids I was hanging out with and attempted to mount the cart to show them what an expert I was with a horse. But the minute I got up on the shaft, Beth bolted and I fell underneath the cart. Lucky it was unloaded, but it ran right over my leg. I ended being rushed to the hospital, thinking my leg was broken. After examination, it turned out my leg was only bruised – just like my ego. Grandad was cross, too, and forbade me to ever go near the horse again.

PART 3

The War

CHAPTER 8

Among falling bombs

I was just nine and I didn't really understand the ins and outs of why we were going to war. What nine-year-old would? I was told we were fighting the enemy, who were the Germans. And all Germans were bastards. All we had to do to the Germans was kill them. It's silly, but what were we to know? And later I found out that the Germans didn't like the Jews and, of course, that was more personal to me as my mother was Jewish, so the Germans wanted to kill my mother and me. I knew that wasn't right. The fact that men were killing each other didn't mean much to us as we used to pretend to do that all the time when we were playing Cowboys and Indians. And that was just a game. As soon as the war started, we pretended to be soldiers, but some of the unfortunate fellas had to pretend to be Germans and they'd be attacked by all of us.

Father had gone off to war. It never occurred to me that he wouldn't come back. That thought didn't even enter my head. It was a peculiar situation. He was the father of six kids and a Territorial Army soldier from this Irish regiment that was the first to be mobilized within days of war being declared. I remember watching as they marched out of the barracks in Chelsea. First of all, they went on manoeuvres, but when they were about to go to North Africa, Father was sent for and told that he wasn't going with the battalion because he had too many children and, at 37, he was seen as being past it. The funny thing is, he actually saw battle before the battalion did because he was posted onto a Dutch ship going backwards and forwards across the Channel taking provisions, arms and ammunitions that the Army needed to survive. He was in charge of all that stuff on board. If there was any danger of the boat being captured, it was his responsibility to blow everything up so that the enemy didn't get it. But, because the Germans knew what the ships were carrying, they bombed them during their journey.

Even though I did have a strong devotion to my father, I don't think I missed him when he was away. I didn't notice his absence at all because there was just so much going on to occupy me. As you've seen, I was very young and a bit of a tearaway – I'd never really been a family person. We were running around, sneaking into places and nicking things, so I was too busy to even give my father a second thought. That was just the way it was. Life was exciting in those days. We made it exciting.

I was also never very close to my siblings at that time. It's funny, I am very close to them now, and to all my children and grandchildren. There's nothing more special than the love you share with your family. But when I was growing up there was no familial bond to speak of. I obviously loved my brothers and sisters, but we didn't really hang out together. If anything, I was happy to be away from them. I liked to do my own thing. To me, they were just little kids whom I'd leave at home or dump as soon as we were out of sight.

I was the big brother and I didn't want to be lumbered with the kids and have them getting in the way.

My brother John was only five when he died. I can't remember the circumstances, but I do remember it was during the war. There were so many illnesses back then that kids were dying all the time. Apparently, I had diphtheria at some point in my life. I don't think anyone knows what that is these days, but it almost killed me, I believe. A lot of kids never survived because some of these illnesses were awful. Some of us survived because we were tough little whatsits, or just lucky, I guess.

London was a dangerous place. We knew what bombs were and, as time went on, we became impervious to those terrible things. One of our games would be to go out of a morning and see who could find the biggest piece of shrapnel. These jagged pieces of metal could tear your hand off. I remember, if a plane had been shot down we would look for the cockpit cover, which was thick Perspex. People made that into jewellery, so we'd shop it around the area and try to sell it. Oh, we were always on the sell. Everything was an adventure. We had no idea what was going on. The Germans would drop incendiary bombs and these deadly anti-personnel ones called Butterfly Bombs. When we saw an incendiary bomb, we'd run and put a sandbag on it. We knew they were fire bombs but we didn't care. On one of the few days I went to school, I saw a bus totally upended, sitting on its back with the engine in the air in Harrington Square. It had been bombed. I don't remember seeing any people on the bus, but we saw bodies quite often, so it wasn't weird for us. At first it was a bit frightening, but eventually you get used to seeing air raid wardens carrying people out of bombed buildings, and bodies lying around the place all the time.

The first time I heard the sirens was frightening. The sound was urgent and haunting, and it immediately made me feel anxious. I'd like to say I was at home when I first heard it, but I can't remember. All I know is when I heard the sound, it put the fear of God in me because I knew what was going to follow. We were going to get bombed and so we had to go to the nearest shelter or get into the Morrison shelter that we had erected in our house.

There were two types of shelter at the time. There was the Anderson shelter, which was made of corrugated, arched iron that you placed into the ground and threw earth over, so it was completely immersed. But most people had the Morrison shelter, which was a cage-like box with a metal plate on top of it to protect those inside. It was always there in the front room and it was big enough for all of us to hide under safely.

But there were other public shelters and, of course, there was the London Underground – I slept down there several times with eiderdowns from home. Those nights were great fun. I don't know how we didn't get pneumonia because it was so blooming cold sometimes. As Father was away, I normally made sure that everyone was rounded up, so we were always together at those times. I never saw any rats or mice, but they were probably too scared to come out with all the bombing going on.

When we heard the bombs dropping, the bangs and booms, we would be very frightened. Sometimes you could hear the sound of the bombs before they made impact, which was even more frightening.

There was this saying: if you could hear the whistle then it's not yours. If there was silence, then it could be yours. The whistle was the sound of the shell going through the air. The deadliest bombs later in the war were the buzz bomb, or doodlebug, and the V-2 rocket. I think I saw the first one that ever dropped. Even now, I feel nervous when I hear aeroplanes flying overhead because I remember that feeling of holding your breath while you waited to see where the bomb was going to land.

The doodlebugs were even more terrifying than the other bombs because they were unmanned and fell everywhere. You'd be at home and hear an aeroplane, and the moment when the engine cut out was horrific because it meant it was about to fall to the ground, exploding and killing people. If we were outside it was even worse because we could see them coming. People would say you should run towards them so they passed over you, but you'd have to be pretty brave to actually do that. But the V-2 rockets were the worst – they were huge and could demolish a whole street of houses. They were big rockets, but they were like little planes, and when they ran out of juice they just dropped. It's not like we could stay in the shelters all the time, so we carried on as much as we could. I used to go and run errands for the air raid wardens.

We would watch wardens and the fire service rooting through bombed buildings, looking for bodies or survivors. When they found something, they would blow on their whistle. Seeing dead bodies soon became an everyday event for us – I remember seeing my first one and just staring at it with morbid fascination. It was part fear, part curiosity – what does that body look like? As it was being carried out of the bombed building, I remember asking the warden, 'Are they dead?' and they said, 'Yes.' I'll never forget seeing the face on the stretcher. It was scary at first because they were lifeless and waxy, and you knew that they really were dead. It was then that I realised what that actually meant – that they weren't going to wake up again.

CHAPTER 9

Escaping country life

Children were evacuated in 1941. All the kids in the area were going, although the lads I hung around with were sent to different places from me. I think some even went as far as Canada, others to Australia. My siblings and I all had our little suitcases with a label on them stating our destination.

I remember that on the train we sat by the window looking out as the green fields whizzed by and I was astonished to see cows. 'Cor, look at that! Cows in the field!' It was quite extraordinary – I'd never seen them before.

When we got to Luton there was a woman on the platform and she told us she was the one who was taking us in. Her name was Mrs Peck and I can't remember too much about her, if I am honest.

Mrs Peck's house was unlike anything we'd ever seen. It was really big, much bigger than my home. She even had a bath, which we were not used to, so we all wanted to have one. I shared my room with three or four boys, but I can't really recall much about them either. There were a few girls there, too, but I wasn't interested in girls – not then anyway.

During that time I was more or less on my own, but I didn't feel lonely. It didn't bother me as I rather liked my own company. I was in another world. I'd never seen cows in a field before, and I loved seeing them as well as the pigs and chickens. I remember trying to find eggs, but the hens pecked at us with a fury! Our legs were pecked to death because we all wore shorts. The air was always smelly, too smelly for me, and I could never work out why people would want to live in the country – it stank. And yet I was very happy being in the stables mucking out, as I was used to doing it for my Grandad. I did find the countryside boring. I loved walking around, discovering what was there, but once I'd seen everything, I just got bored. London was much more interesting. Much more exciting.

There were these red berries that caught my eye and I wondered what they tasted like. They tasted very nice but they were actually elderberries and they could have killed me. Fortunately, I was violently sick, but I don't know how many of them I'd eaten. In those days I didn't know the danger, I was just an ignorant kid. Then I came across a field with plants that I realised were carrots. They looked ready to eat, so I pulled them out and wiped the mud off on my jersey.

After a few days, I realised I didn't like this quiet country life and decided that I wanted to go back to London, even though it was being bombed by the enemy. I just wanted to be back at home for some reason – it was what I knew – so one night I snuck away from the house, leaving all my belongings behind. I headed to the road that would take me back to London to hitch a ride, but no one would stop for me, so I had to wait for some trucks to slow down and then jump aboard. You can see that I had left the house with no real plan. All I knew was that London was in that direction. Of course, I was a kid on his own, so if anyone had actually stopped for me, they'd have asked why I was so intent on going back to London, so I made up an elaborate story. The last thing I wanted them to think was that I was on the run. It sounds hard to imagine now, but I got back to London in three days and made my way through the streets to home. When I got there, Mother was very surprised to see me, but she didn't tell me off. I think she was rather glad that I was back to help her carry out some errands and she swiftly got me working around the place.

Towards the end of the war, in about 1944, my grandparents moved to Coventry. They were on war work. Nan was assistant cook in the kitchen of a factory while Grandad Tom was a labourer. My parents would eventually divorce once the war was over. When it happened, I was living temporarily with my grandparents in Coventry, just before I joined the Army.

CHAPTER 10

Family bonds

I make it sound as if Father didn't have much to do with me or my siblings, but that's not entirely true. Albert was a great dad, but he had other things on his plate. He worked hard, he was in the Territorial Army, and he was away for long periods of the Second World War. When his marriage came to an end, my brothers and sisters were taken away from Mother by the local authority and he wasn't really given the choice of looking after them because men weren't given custody in those days. It was believed that children needed a woman's touch, so fathers rarely got a look-in.

I don't know why my siblings weren't sent to my grandparents, bearing in mind I had practically lived with Nan and Grandad on and off for years. Instead, the kids were packed off to a woman called Mrs Pilbeam, who lived in Hastings.

Brian, the youngest of the lot, was only a baby when all this happened, so he never even knew our mother, which is strange when you think about it. He didn't actually see much of me either, for that matter, because by the time they were banished to the coast, I was with relations, then busy being a soldier, travelling abroad and getting married. Heavens, I didn't even invite them to my wedding which, looking back, I do feel bad about.

When I was away in Boys' Service, Father would write to me all the time. We had a good relationship and he did try to make an effort with me, but he just wasn't around all that much. I would come to understand this once I was in the Army and saw how much of your life it takes up.

But Father and I would see each other whenever we could. I wasn't allowed out of Boys' Service for the first six weeks, but when I finally was let out, I went up to London from Woolwich to see him. He was still serving at that time, so we didn't have much time to see each other. I remember, when I arrived at the station, he was waiting for me at the end of the platform. I strolled up to him and I could tell that he was taking me in, with my smart uniform – I had spent all morning working on it so it looked all pressed and fresh. 'Hello son,' he said with a sarcastic smile. 'There's only one man in the British Isles who can wear his hat on the side of his head – and that's the Prince of Wales.' He gave me a gentle clip around my head and said, 'Put your hat on straight.'

Later on, he would tell me that he was very proud of me when I signed up to Boys' Service. It wasn't just that he was worried I would end up in Borstal; he also thought that, underneath my Jack-the-lad exterior, I was a talented drummer and potentially a very good soldier.

I felt sorry for Father. I knew his relationship with Mother had been tough for years and I think he was relieved when it came to an end. All they ever did was fight and I don't think he knew what she was up to when he was away. Nan and Aunty Maisie were always going on at him about how they didn't think she was good enough for him and, when it eventually ended – while I was staying with my grandparents in Coventry – I think he felt relieved that it was all over. I sense that he was angry with himself, blaming himself for letting the unhappy marriage go on for so long.

In spite of Mother's behaviour, I have to admit I do feel sorry for her too. When I explained her story to Joan, she reminded me that she had become a mum at 15 years old – 15! She was just a young slip of a lass, who'd been disowned by her entire family and married at 16 without any kind of life. For heaven's sake, she wasn't old enough to have experienced one. I'm not making excuses for her, but I can see that she did have a lot to contend with and so many issues that a child her age shouldn't have had to deal with. And let's not forget she was from a wealthy Jewish family and had married into a poor working-class family. God, it was never going to work, was it?

The breakdown of Mother and Father's relationship is still a bit of a mystery to me. I was rarely at home and neither Mother nor Father ever told me about the problems they had with each other. This was at a time when kids and parents didn't have the kind of relationships we have now. Mums and dads didn't talk about the inner workings of their marriage to the kids. It was unheard of. It was when I went to stay with my grandparents in Coventry that the split occurred and so details are rather sparse. To be honest, I felt quite removed from the whole affair and have never since asked Father about what actually happened between them. I didn't think it was my business and a lot of water had passed under the bridge.

It would be years later that I would be reunited with my siblings and it was my father who managed to bring the clan back together again. Father had been in constant touch with the children all this time and had squeezed in visits whenever he could. I vaguely remember going to see them once or twice myself. It wasn't long after they'd moved to Hastings, but I think I stopped pretty smartish when I got swept up into army life.

When we all met up for the first time, we were all a bit wary of each other. Well, they were wary of me and I guess I was unsure of them, which was not a surprise really. We were practically strangers, bonded only by blood. Why should the fact that we shared the same parents mean that we hit it off straightaway? I remember the first meeting was very awkward. They weren't sure how to deal with me, or what to say. But we muddled through and, as the years went by, we got closer and closer and forged a strong relationship, seeing much more of each other at family functions such as weddings and the like.

I was pleased to hear that my siblings' lives had proved to be fruitful after such an inauspicious start. Brian had been in the Army for 30 years and went from Boys' Service to become a lieutenant colonel. We never actually crossed paths when he was in Boys' Service as he was in a different regiment, the Royal Electrical and Mechanical Engineers. Maisie became a nurse and later married a policeman. Mike also joined the Army and went to the King's Troop but was sadly invalided out of the service when a horse fell on him. He didn't let that incident put him off and went on to become a territorial soldier and, later, a mental health nurse. Shirley also joined the Army. In fact, she was one of the first women to sign up to WRAC (the Women's Royal Army Corps), previously known as the Auxiliary Territorial Society. She didn't last all that long as a soldier and became an army wife instead, marrying one of my friends!

About ten years after his divorce, Father announced, out of the blue, that he was planning to get married again and wanted me to be his best man. I was a sergeant with a reserve regiment in Yorkshire at the time so had to ask my commanding officer for permission for special leave. When I asked him if I could have time off for my father's wedding, he burst into a fit of laughter and said, 'Now that's not something I hear every day. Of course, you can.' I think he was still laughing as I left the office.

Father said that he had found someone to love and I was really happy for him. I hoped that whoever he was marrying would give him whatever it was that Mother couldn't.

One of my biggest regrets in life is that I didn't try to search for my mother. When she left, I didn't hear another word about her again. It was as if she had disappeared from the face of the Earth. I think for a while I was angry that she had just left. Then I got so caught up with the Army and my own family that I simply forgot about her.

It wasn't until a few decades later that I did finally find out something about Mother. I'd received a note from the Prudential insurance company to inform me that Father, who had died in November 1966, had taken out a 'penny policy' and that it had matured over the years. They said if I could give them proof that I was his son, they would send us the money. Once that was sorted,

I asked the person on the phone to see if my mother had also set up a penny policy. Bingo! She had, though it turned out she had only left £7 in the account. I had to find evidence that she had died and, after a search, I tracked down her death certificate, which informed me she had died on 20 April 1974.

Combining Mother's sum with Father's, I attended my brother Brian's sixtieth birthday in Grantham, Lincolnshire, and gave him £100, telling him it was a gift from our mother and father, and we bought as much booze with it as we could.

CHAPTER 11

Boys' Service

I dread to think of the life that could have been waiting for me if I hadn't joined the Army. I had been a tearaway and could see myself ending up in enormous amounts of trouble. Trouble to make your eyes water. Run-ins with the police had become the norm for me, but there was one time I was stopped by a policeman – an inspector – and he was different. He was a huge fella, very intimidating, and he already knew of me (they all did), but I recall that he was less terrifying than the usual coppers and much kinder. He did me the favour of giving me an option that no one had before. He said, 'You can carry on getting into scrapes and end up in Borstal or you can join the Army and do something with your life.' My father was in the Army and I was excited because I had always dreamed about being a soldier, I just didn't think I had it in me. For the first time, I felt like I was making the right decision and that I had a purpose.

A little while later, in 1945, when I was in Coventry staying with my grandparents, Grandad took me down to the recruitment office, which was nerve-wracking but also exciting. I told them, 'I want to be a marine,' but the fella said there were no vacancies at that time and that I'd have to wait six months. Well, I was desperate to get in there and start, so they offered me the Royal Artillery instead and so I said, 'Okay, let's go!' Easy as that. It's funny because Grandad spelt my name wrong on the form – Thackeray instead of Thackery – and we didn't realise until some months later when a problem arose in the Army records. Father was sent for and had to sort it out, but nevertheless, I was in.

The next thing I knew, I was sent down to London on my own and I had to report to a place called the Army Academy in Woolwich. I was told to sit in the guardroom – a cold and uninviting place, and altogether quite scary. I heard the gates clanging shut after me and it felt as if I was being locked up forever. I thought I was tough back then, but in these new surroundings I felt very small and very naïve. I realised that maybe I didn't know what I was letting myself in for. The guards, the gates – I imagined that's how prison felt. But then someone fetched me and took me to F Troop. I walked into the barrack room with all these other boys filing in who had just signed up like me. Seeing them put me at ease. I wasn't nervous any more because they looked like ordinary boys. Boys like me. I was allotted my bed space and given my Army number – 1157710. That's the only thing we had to learn and the one thing that stays with any Army man until the day he dies. You never forget your Army number. It was my new badge of honour.

Without a second thought, we were told what to do. It wasn't a long list – keep everything clean, keep your bed space clear and generally do as you're told. I picked up my full uniform. We had what were called denims, made of denim material but khaki in colour and with brass buttons. That's when they gave us the shortest short back and sides. That came as a bit of a shock to many of us, to lose most of our hair, but I didn't mind it. In later years, they stopped cutting hair quite so short like that because the boys ended up looking like skinheads but, back in the day, we were like little short-haired replicas of each other.

There was always someone in charge of the barrack room – an NCO, which stood for non-commissioned officer. There were boy NCOs, but they had little power. Most of the powers came from the senior NCO – a bombardier or a sergeant. In those days they all had war medal ribbons as they had been in the Army for some time. They ruled our lives, but they did so with such differing styles. Our troop sergeant was a hoot. Charlie Wilshire was his name and he was a character. He would walk into the dorm, throw his battledress at one of us and demand that we get the stripes whitened. Someone would be assigned to do his boots and brasses and if the work wasn't good enough, he'd tick you off. You did not want a ticking off from Charlie Wilshire. He commanded respect so we always did what we were told. But because we liked him, we used to take the mickey out of him too, with silly little pranks and comments, and he was game for it. Funnily enough, long after we had all left the Army, we invited Charlie to one of our Boys' Service reunions. He must have been in his nineties but he still called us his boys. We were grandads by that time and he was too. He'd had nine children and was ever so old when he eventually died.

I felt lucky because all in all I settled into the artillery pretty quickly. I certainly didn't miss home because I'd found a structure that worked for me. The discipline and regimented days suited me.

We'd get up at 6.30am to the sound of a trumpet. There was time for a quick shower, to brush your teeth and shave if you needed to. We were young, but at the first sign of some fluff on your face, you had to become accustomed to the razor pretty quickly. For me, that came not too long after joining, which was nice. It added to my feeling of developing from boy to man.

It wasn't just us that had to be spotless though. We laid out our bed space for inspection – everything had to be absolutely pristine. The bed tidied and made up, the blankets all lined up and folded in a special way, your kit all laid out, loos and sinks cleaned and floors shiny. To get the floors shiny enough to eat your dinner off, you put down this old-fashioned Mansion polish and you had a bumper, which was a rather heavy brush with a long pole. You would run it up and down with a cloth under it. The more weight you put on it, the more shine you got, so you would sit the smallest boy on the bumper and he would be pushed up and down. This all had to be done before 8.30am. If you left your area untidy, you were on fatigues (punishment duty) that night, which is why you rapidly got into the habit of tidiness. Inspections were of paramount importance. That is why it is difficult to get out of those kind of habits, even at my age now, although that isn't such a bad thing, I suppose.

At 8.30am, we were called on parade, when you were inspected and marched off to do various things: a gun drill, a marching drill and a rifle drill, among others. Gun drill was very important and extremely strict. We took posts on a 25-pounder, a field gun that fired a shell weighing 25 pounds, hence the name. It was a huge thing mounted on a firing platform and carriage, so we'd have six men on the job and take turns on the different posts, learning each job and ultimately how to fire the thing. Rifle drill and gun drill is what a boy dreams about when he joins the Army and I'm pleased to say shooting the rifles and handguns on the military ranges lived up to expectation. We'd fire a small rifle called a .22, which is a small calibre, and aim at targets set up on a range of about fifty yards. It was great fun. It was a good starting point for an enthusiastic boy and I was a reasonable shot, but when you were senior you got to go on a range and fire a much bigger rifle, which was exhilarating. A few steps up from firing corks with my pop gun as a kid! In my teenage years I would dream about going to war. Some might struggle to understand that but this was what we were trained to do, so putting it into action was what we aspired to. We treated it like playing cowboys; you knew in your heart that when you saw the cowboy had been shot he was not really dead. Later on, I'd come to know the heartbreak of war, but for now I was eager to learn and do my bit.

If you were good at everything at drill, you could join the band and I did this as soon as I had the opportunity. I had already developed a love of military bands, having watched Father leading bands when I was a youngster. Our band comprised of a cavalry trumpet, bugle and drums. Everyone was taught to play and traditionally the young ones blew the trumpet. I could play the trumpet but I was always a drummer. In the days after initial training, when the boys used to be on their regular units, they would keep time and alert the soldiers to lunch, dinner or parade by sounding the correct call. Marching was a huge part of everyday life in service – we would march everywhere. There was a knack to it, plus it was important to keep your right hand free and swinging in case you had to salute. Even these days I automatically salute the captains or the ladies at the Hospital, but only when I'm in uniform.

One requirement of my day that I was surprised to have embraced as I did was school. The boys had to do half a day, every day, of academic education. I was hesitant as I'd had poor schooling and I was told by my superiors that I needed to knuckle down if I was to achieve higher ranks. So I did just that and studied maths, English and map reading. I was okay, I certainly wasn't stupid, but my school age was probably equivalent to a nine- or ten-year-old with an ability for simple sums and reasonable writing. I'm grateful for my love of reading because, due to the cowboy books and books about soldiers that I had read from cover to cover, my spelling was up to scratch. Working hard and getting my exams enabled me to get my third-class certificate of education, which you needed to become an NCO, and then after that my second and ultimately my first, which you needed if you had designs on becoming a sergeant major.

Weekends brought a different schedule – no schooling for starters – but inspections didn't stop. On Saturdays there was the battery commander's inspection and he looked at every minute thing. Now this was an important event because passing that inspection meant you could go out on a Saturday night. There was a fierce competition between the troops in the battery – I think there were six; A to F – and between rooms. There were around 20 boys in a barrack room. You would stand by the right of your bed – that was the order – and you would have to lay out every single piece of equipment you had, two of everything and spare boots. They were polished on top and underneath, and the 13 studs in each boot were also cleaned. We used to lay out our polish tins – brown for belt, black for boots, tins of Brasso, our cleaning rags, everything you owned. Later on, when we got sheets, which were a luxury, they had to be folded in a certain way. I was not bad at this, I have to admit. Everything you owned, including your toothbrush, toothpaste and housewife – which was a sewing and repair kit – had to be neat. This took so long that we actually used to lay it out before we went to bed and then sleep on the floor, so that when we got up in the morning it was immaculate. As daft as it sounds, we used to do that every Friday night. To get one over on the next room or the next troop, we would get the polish tins, scrape all the paint off the tins and polish them, so you had two silver tins on your bed and a Brasso bottle. We thought this looked better than the original painted tins. It was bonkers in hindsight, but that's the way it was. I can't say I'm a regimental dad with my own kids, but I think there is some military-learned behaviour that I can't shake, such as the cleanliness and tidiness. My children went to school with clean shoes, which I would do for them when they were young and then I taught them how to do it to military standard. My son is 59 now and turns himself out very well. He did a couple of years in the RAF.

As with any job, there were some guys I disliked intensely and I kept away from them. I hadn't been there long when I gave some lip to a guy in the washroom. He took offence and I ended up on my back, lying on the washroom floor. I got back on my feet and took him on again, but he floored me again. I didn't realise at the time that he was a welterweight boxing champion! The extraordinary thing was that in later life he was posted to my regiment as a lance bombardier, but this time there were no fisticuffs.

Washroom disagreements aside, most of the guys I liked. My best friend there was called Horton. He was a great lad and we became firm friends. Funnily enough, I was introduced one day to a lady at the Royal Hospital Chelsea, who saw my regimental belt and said, 'I see you were in the Royal Artillery. My father joined the Royal Artillery when he was just a little boy and, before the end of Boys' Service, he transferred into the Horse Guards.' I knew right away who she was or, I should say, who her father was, so I said, 'Your name must be Horton'. Not many boys were transferred by their father or older sibling into a different unit.

Despite the discipline in Woolwich, we did take risks. For instance, occasionally we would bunk out of the barracks. This was highly illegal as far as the Army was concerned. Juniors had to be in by 10pm, 10.30pm for seniors. You had to book in, otherwise you would be marked absent and they would send the military police out for you. It was not an easy feat to sneak out. The barracks were old-fashioned with tall iron railings all around and any brick walls had broken glass on the top. We discovered there was part of the wall where you could make it over relatively unscathed, but for the odd cut or bruise, and those of us in the know would put on our denim overalls and sneak out without cap badges or anything, just gym shoes.

Once safely over, we went down to the Woolwich ferry, which used to run overnight, sneak on and keep an eye open for people on the lookout for stray soldiers. On the other side of the river,

The only pre-war shot of me
I own, *c.* 1935.

Boys' Service,
in London, *c.* 1946.

F Troop, Boys' Battery, Royal Artillery. I'm sitting on a chair front row, far right.

Joan Gornall at the age of 17, in 1947.

The girl who caught my eye.
Joan at the age of 19, in 1950.

The newly wed couple - Mr and Mrs Thackery, September, 1950.

The wedding party. From left to right: Henry (Joan's brother), me, Joan, Adele (Joan's sister), Norman (her father), Alice (Joan's mother) and Bert (my father).

In Korea, as part of the concert party, standing outside
the theatre.

Above left and right: 14th Regiment survey party on patrol in the New Territories, Hong Kong.

Me with a cavalry trumpet. I had to learn Chinese calls on it in order to play them to the Chinese troops as a victory call on the capture of any enemy position. Here I'm using it to sound a fanfare at the reopening of the British Legation following the recapturing of Seoul.

Above and below: On patrol in the New Territories, Hong Kong.
I took the photograph above. I am grimacing at the taste of hard rations in the photograph below – which is probably why the chap on the right is laughing!

Joan, our maid Margaret (centre) and her friend Ah Ying, in Hong Kong.

The Hong Kong Archery Club. Joan and I were founder members and Joan was the First Lady Paramount (Club Champion). Here she's kneeling 3rd from the right; I'm taking the photo.

Joan and Dawn in Hong Kong.

Grandad Tom and Dawn.

Aunty Maisie and Dawn.

Joan and me doing what we loved best – dancing the night away.

we would earn a little money by washing bottles in the Express Dairy overnight. We used to load up these machines with the old milk bottles and we worked for most of the night for just a few shillings, which wasn't much. But whatever it was, it was money in our pockets, which felt good, and we would then sneak back in again. On the odd occasion boys were caught, security would be increased on the escape route and nobody would creep out for a while. But soon enough, the beefed-up security would die down and you could sneak out again. It was a waiting game for cheeky fellas like me.

Luckily, I never got caught. If I had, I would have been up on multiple charges – absent without leave, improperly dressed, escaping without permission, sneaking over the wall – and I would have gone up before the troop commander, then the battery commander and then I'd have been sentenced. Those unlucky enough to be caught found themselves locked in the small guardroom that acted as a barracks prison. There, you'd be under close inspection and have to do all sorts of chores, such as peeling potatoes for dinner and cleaning pots. There was another punishment that was particular to our Boys' Service, which was called 'hoxters'. We all got this at one time or another. Hoxters meant you were confined to barracks and at regular intervals during the evening you would be sent to the guard commander and he would send you to carry out all kinds of jobs. It wasn't a serious punishment, though; I can't remember being in serious trouble ever.

Yes, we sneaked out every now and again, but everyone did it. It was harmless and nobody got hurt. But we didn't leave the barracks just for washing bottles; we'd also attend dances at the local Labour Club, where we'd pay sixpence on the door. We needed that time away to let off steam on a Saturday night after regimented days with strict discipline. We were always in uniform, never civilian clothes, but we took our cap badge off and put it in our pockets because girls were notorious for stealing cap badges to make into belts, as was a fashion of the time. For me, it was always about the dancing. Well, you daren't touch alcohol because they would smell it on your breath when you returned and next thing you knew you would be sent to the guardroom. I always impressed my friends with my moves because none of them could dance – they would just stand at the sides, smirking and smoking. That wasn't my thing; after all, we were at a dance, plus there were girls. I was straight in there on the dance floor and I always got the girls. For reasons I never understood, they seemed to flock around me – maybe they liked my moves too – but the romances were just a kiss goodnight and never anything more. I met some sweet girls on Saturday nights but, on the whole, they just weren't all that important during my army life.

On other occasions, we would go to the Woolwich Empire to unwind, where they had variety shows featuring the lovely blonde pin-up of the time, Chrystabel 'Jane' Leighton-Porter. She played a burlesque character called Jane, who started life as a comic strip in the *Daily Mirror* newspaper but who later was brought to life on stage. I can't remember too much of what she did, except turn up and not wear that many clothes. She set a few hearts beating, I can tell you. We could only afford to go up into the gods and peer over the top of the balcony, but we were mesmerized by this lady – you should've seen her!

We were paid weekly, but it didn't amount to much. We'd get half a guinea, which was ten and sixpence a week, but five shillings of that was automatically deducted into savings so that when you went on leave, you had some money. That gave you five shillings in your hand – it's hilarious to think that's only 25p in today's money! Despite the tiny sum, it was usually enough as we didn't want for much. The odd sixpence would pay for haircuts, but we did spend money on cigarettes, particularly Woodbines, which was the cigarette of choice back then. We could afford to buy them in packets of five and at first they made me feel sick, but everyone was doing it so you'd try one, then try another and next thing you're a smoker. It sounds funny now because times have changed so much, but smoking was very important to us because it was so fashionable. I remember smoking my five at a café called Shirley's just outside Cambridge Barracks. You knew you could get a good feed there – we called it a belly filler. My order was bread pudding with thick lumps and a huge mug of hot sweet tea on the side, each costing a penny. But if we'd had a costly week and didn't have the money, we could pay Shirley another time. She was good like that to us boys.

We may not have earned much money, but we did well for good grub. Closer to home, the Officers' Mess in Woolwich was another great dining experience. I believe it's the oldest and certainly, in my opinion, one of the most beautiful messes in the Army. We would walk there, in the middle of the parade ground, and report to the mess sergeant. We'd stand either side of the stairs and sound two calls – the half-an-hour call and a five-minute call. Then, once everyone was in, we'd sound the mess call, which was a tricky one as it had to be played in unison. Then the mess sergeant would clap, make everyone sit down inside, then say, 'Off you go', which meant we could go to the kitchen and stuff our faces with food. They had officers' mess dinners every month, but I think I did it four times.

Aside from the eating, dancing and free time, I enjoyed sport, and physical training was taken every day with an instructor. That meant a lot of gym work, such as ropes, the horse and the wall bars, and luckily, despite being beefier than some of the other boys, I was agile. I have always been on the heavy side but I was active and very fit back then, plus the PT programme got tougher as you went on so you would improve. We used medicine balls, the heavy leather balls that are thrown at you and would literally knock you over. I got a few bruises from those. Ball games were a big part of PT and we would enjoy assigning teams and getting fiercely competitive with each other. One time, we were exercising, when all of a sudden we heard this great yell and out of the office of the gym came this tall sergeant major in full battledress. He lay down on the floor on his back in front of us all, then went up onto his shoulders and did a backflip, landing on the toes of his army boots. We watched in awe. He got up like it was nothing and said to the boys, 'This is what I want from you all.' Well, who were we to argue? I ran into him sitting in the lounge of a troop ship years later. By then he had been commissioned and was a captain, and I reminded him of his physical spectacle and we laughed.

Sadly, what I boasted in fitness and agility, I lacked in boxing. I so wanted to be good at boxing because I loved it. My father, who had been an army flyweight, watched one particular bout of mine and said, 'You might as well pack that up.' I wasn't tall enough, I was too heavy and I didn't have the reach he had. I was fighting as a light heavyweight and I competed within the battery and against other boys' units, but I was often knocked out and won nothing. In comparison, Father had cups all over the place – he was only 5ft 3in but a scrappy and talented fighter. It was a shame not to make him proud with my boxing.

I had been in the Boys' Service for almost two years when the end of the war came and we took part in the 1946 victory parades. It was a privilege for us boy soldiers to honour the soldiers returning from active duty. We felt such elation and excitement as we lined the steps of Mansion House in London. It was the first time many of us had ever stayed in a hotel. Ours was in Baker Street and we slept in sheets, which felt like heaven, and we had breakfast in the kitchen. We thought it was rather posh for ordinary lads like us, like we'd been promoted to royal status or something. There were big celebrations at the Royal Albert Hall. Since I played the bass drum in the band, I was selected to stand in the middle of the auditorium at the Royal Albert Hall in pitch black and, with a cavalry trumpet at the ready, the spotlight would come down upon me and I would play a fanfare, leading a sixty-piece trumpet band marching into the centre of the auditorium. As soon as I finished the last note, I had to dash off stage to get on my bearskin hat and rush back on, belting away at my bass drum. I had a lot of pressure on my young shoulders, but I loved it.

Of course, that was the enjoyable side and one I felt privileged to have been a part of, but the other side of war is the stark reality of death. One of our jobs in the band was to play when the bodies were brought back and buried at Brookwood Military Cemetery in Surrey. If you were a good trumpet sounder, as I was, you'd get drafted in wearing the full gear, including the busby hat and jacket you see on the King's Troop Royal Horse Artillery, out of respect to the soldier. The coffin would be carried in and you'd go down with the trumpet majors. It was an altogether extremely sombre affair and it was here that you'd realise what war meant, that you might not come home and see your family and loved ones ever again. Or, if you were one of the luckier ones, you'd come home injured but alive. I saw all sides and I'm grateful for the outlook it's given me and the experience I've taken through the rest of my years.

CHAPTER 12

The Royal Artillery

In two short years, I had transformed myself from a right little tinker causing havoc on the streets of Camden to a slightly more responsible young soldier. The training and the education I received during my time in the Boys' Service was invaluable and had broadened my mind good and proper. It was scary to think that if I'd carried on the way I was going, I could have been banged up in Borstal, mixing with the wrong crowd and learning how to become more of a reprobate. But my time in Woolwich was soon coming to an end and I was looking forward to new opportunities that were opening up to me. Little did I know that my next step would take me on a rather exciting adventure that I could never have imagined.

One Saturday, all three-hundred boys from the battery were taking part in one of the regular Saturday parades. The band, with every member looking his finest, was out in full force marching around the grounds in tight formation. I was on the bass drum, wearing a bearskin. As we did a circuit, a high-ranking officer I'd never seen before stepped out onto the parade ground and joined our officers. Together, they all kept a very watchful eye on proceedings, paying close attention to the band in particular and occasionally whispering to each other. Eventually, our commanding officer called a halt and we all assumed our positions. The group of men paced up and down in front of us scrutinizing each and every one of us with every step. By now we knew that we had to be turned out smart and polished so, unless they were looking for minuscule details that the naked eye would barely pick up, I felt confident that I had nothing to worry about. Still, the officers continued to survey the group, creating a tension that you could feel rippling across the rest of the troops like dominos.

Then this new man broke the silence and said, 'Thackery, take the bass drum off and put a side drum on and march forward.'

Oh, good lord, I thought, what I have done now? Was I in hot water? What have these fellas got in store for me? Immediately shrugging off any fears, I did what I was told, marched confidently towards them and swapped drums.

The new chap, who was an oddly petite man with a moustache, stepped forward and looked at me, the expression on his face giving nothing away.

'Play a paradiddle, play a roll, march up and down with the drum,' the little colonel barked. I wasn't quite sure what was going on, but I was content in the knowledge that I was rather proficient at the task I was being set.

As ordered, I performed the paradiddle, then the roll, while marching up and down. All sounded good, as far as I was concerned. I stole a side glance at the little colonel but still couldn't gauge what he was thinking. Stony faced, he simply eyeballed me, glancing up and down and taking me all in. He and the other officers all leaned in for an inaudible conflab before breaking free again.

Then the little fella said to the officers, 'Yes I'll take him'.

I was confused. Take me? Take me where?

I was told to step forward and my officers formally introduced me to this new chap. His name was Colonel Owen Geary, and he was the principal director of music of the Royal Artillery. He explained to me that he was on the hunt for a drummer boy for one of their bands and he thought I was simply perfect for the role.

Ah, now all seemed clear. Being pulled out of the parade was an audition of sorts to see if I had the skills to join the prestigious RA band. The RA band dated back to the 1700s and had a long tradition for entertaining the troops in their camps around the world. I was ecstatic that I was being offered such an extraordinary opportunity, especially as I was only 16 and there was still at least a year before my time in Boys' Service was officially completed.

With no further ado, I packed up my gear, said goodbye to the fellas and was posted to the artillery band based at Larkhill, Salisbury.

When I arrived at the new barracks I reported immediately to the sergeant major so that he could explain what was expected of me. Standing before him in his office, clad in my khaki uniform, leather belt and chin strap, polished and shiny. I could sense he was looking me up and down. And then he said, 'Well, you can stop that straightaway,' nodding at my perfectly turned-out attire. 'We don't do bull in the band, we just clean things. Stop all the spit and polish, you'll put everyone to shame.'

I wanted to chuckle, but chose not to. The sergeant major then went on to explain that as part of the band I would be joining them on an overseas tour. This was amazing news. The furthest I'd ever been in my life was, so far, up north, when the Boys' Service took part in a recruiting tour, so to imagine that was I about to take to the high seas and see the world was simply astonishing for me. Among the places we were due to visit were Malta, Gibraltar, Egypt, the Middle East, the Far East, Sri Lanka, Singapore and Hong Kong. If I'm honest, I'd heard of some of these countries, but for the life of me I couldn't possibly tell you where they were on a map, so I was looking forward to embarking on some wild adventures. What more could a 16-year-old lad with once limited prospects possibly want?

Sadly, my time with the band wasn't exactly a walk in the park. The rest of the fellas were much older than me and were a combination of National Service men, a lot of whom came from the old brass bands in the north or the Salvation Army. I was the youngest so found it hard to bridge the gap with the other fellas. For the first few weeks I was left on my own quite a lot of the time as the others were off doing jobs. This gave me a lot of alone time and I wondered whether this was the actually best direction for me to be taking. But the Royal Artillery band had an illustrious past that dated back hundreds of years, so I'd be a fool to even think about stepping away.

What I couldn't work out was why I had been chosen in the first place. For one, I was young with very little life or military experience and for another, there were already two drummers in the band who'd known each other for years and had served together during the last war.

Over time, however, I slowly developed a stronger bond with the other men so that when we did eventually set off around the world, I didn't feel quite so isolated.

At this point in time, troops would be transported across the world by troop ship, which was an incredibly slow process. The ships were owned by civilian companies, but the Army would take over the liner and install a regimental sergeant major, a ship commandant and various other officers.

To say the journey was boring was an understatement. It took practically a month to reach anywhere, which meant a lot of us started to go stir crazy almost as soon as we embarked on our journey. But there were ways of alleviating the boredom. We could eat, exercise and run around the decks.

But what I would mostly do was stand up on the deck and look out to sea. Simple as it sounds, I was mesmerized to see how big the world actually was. I was so used to the cluttered streets of London or the confines of an army barracks that to see the wide, open sea was something quite extraordinary to me. Even if there was nothing to take in but the open sea and the wonderful sight of dolphins and flying fish, it was not wasted on me just how the big the world actually was. I really was quite blown away by it all. Even to see the waves crashing around the ship was an experience for me. Up until now, I had only ever been to the seaside once and to see all this water – well, it was all so new to me.

CHAPTER 12

Seeing the world

When we docked in Malta, we had the choice of staying aboard ship or going ashore. During the journey I had got to know these two percussionists who had been there before. They asked me if I fancied tagging along. Lumbered with the choice of staying on the ship, bored out of my mind, or seeing a bit of a new town in Malta, I didn't hesitate in accepting their offer.

They took me to a place called Strait Street in Valletta, known affectionately to the soldiers as the 'Gut'. It was anything but picturesque. A rough-and-ready narrow street in the seedy part of Valletta, it was dark and oppressive because the buildings on either side of the road were so tall that it was hard for daylight to penetrate. Strait Street really came alive after dark when the doors to the bars, jazz clubs, restaurants and bordellos were thrown open. It was, my companion explained, the place where every British and American serviceman would go to on their shore leave to find all sorts of shenanigans. The locals were a mix of nationalities, social classes and folks from all walks of life and, as we started along the street, I could see first-hand that this was a rowdy and sleazy place where anything goes. Drinks flowed endlessly, fights broke out between drunk soldiers, ladies of the night plied their trade in doorways and cross-dressers prowled the length of the street on the lookout for any military men who dared to try something new. It was grubby and grotesque, for sure, but, to a teenager like me, also one of the most exciting places I had ever seen. Not that I can remember too much, of course. No sooner were we on the strip than the lads were on a mission to have a good time! Which we did. While we hopped from one bar to the next, I noticed that some of the working women appeared to take rather a shine to me, probably because I looked so young and was taller and beefier than some of the other guys I'd seen. I had already spied various drunk and randy servicemen surreptitiously slipping into doorways with women and fancied a bit of action myself (you know, when in Valletta!). But my two mates weren't having any of it and made sure they kept me close at hand. They were wise fellas indeed, warning me about sampling the local delights that could have left me with a nasty case of the clap. Instead, the blighters took us further down the 'Gut', which seemed to become darker and more oppressive and where the bars looked grubbier and sleazier. We ended up in one that was run by two beefy gay guys, who were slathered in badly applied make-up. Bear in mind, this was a time when homosexuality was illegal back home in England and you didn't tend to mix in those circles. So back then, in my naïve, uneducated frame of mind, these two men scared the living daylights out of me – and my two mates, who knew them, thought it was a huge laugh. I think the two gay chaps could sense my unease and cheekily took advantage by squeezing me in between them and proceeding to behave in what I think you'd describe as a flirtatious manner. After a little while, the two guys both started sniggering and admitted they had only been pulling my leg, which was a relief. They turned out to be a couple of top blokes, who continued to keep me and my mates in drinks and lewd stories about curious soldiers until the three of us could take no more and decided to stagger back, arm in arm, to the ship.

The next stop was Egypt, which I must say looked unlike any place I'd ever seen. The temperature was ferocious, the streets were more cramped and less, dare I say, sophisticated and the people had darker skin than I was used to seeing back home. It sounds naïve to say something like that in this day and age, but bear in mind that back then I had seen little, if anything, of life overseas or of any foreigners. We didn't have access to as much media as we do now.

When we settled in our tented camp, we spent ages unloading our instruments, which were numerous and heavy. As I was one of the strongest and fittest among the party, I happily spent most of the blazing-hot day lugging the weighty stuff around, noticing much too late that I'd been pretty much left to do it on my own by the other guys. By early evening, I was literally dripping with sweat and my muscles were aching. Observing that I was in a bit of an unsightly state, one of the lads suggested I go and cool off in the pool along the way, which sounded like a great idea. So, I dashed to the pool, stripping everything off, and threw myself in, expecting to land in refreshing, cool water. But what I'd forgotten to take into consideration was the massive temperature drop when the sun packed up for the day. The moment I hit the water, I wanted to scream. It was freezing and it felt like I was jumping into a pit of knives. Well aware that I'd been played for a fool by the older men, I knew I couldn't react and show weakness, so I simply continued to splash around gleefully until those who had gathered around the pool grew tired of seeing me not react and dispersed.

Unlike in Malta, we didn't really venture out to the local places. I was keen, of course, because I was thirsty to see new places, new cultures and different kinds of people. But when I asked if we could hit the local areas, I was advised against it because it was the kind of place a naïve young soldier could easily be taken advantage of, and so we didn't.

Of all the stop-offs, I think Sri Lanka was my favourite. Known back then as Ceylon, it was the closest to paradise I had ever been. The sun was strong, the heat was intense and it looked like the kind of place you'd see in the pictures. To get to the next camp, all our gear was piled onto three-tonne trucks, which carried us from Colombo through the jungle to the military base in Trincomalee in the Eastern province. The sights I saw over those days are ingrained in my memory forever. I saw working elephants for the first time and was genuinely stunned by their bulk and leathery skin. I also remember these vivid red flowers in the jungle, which appeared to glow almost like neon lights, courtesy of the blazing sun against the rich green foliage.

At the camp, the band put on a rousing show for the troops who had been posted to Trincomalee months before. It was a great camp, as we had a stage to perform on, and we could see from the soldiers' faces during our three days of performances that we were just the light relief they had been waiting for.

Staying at these camps was actually a lot of fun and, as we got to know the troops we were visiting, we became part of their world. On our tour, rumours had started circulating that I had a bit of a voice so I was constantly being asked to get up and sing, which I was only too happy to do, usually crooning ballads.

After Ceylon, we stopped off in Hong Kong and Malaya (now Malaysia), two very beautiful and exotic locations. Kuala Lumpur was where you went for fun and frolics, and didn't we just! One of the few vague memories I have is of going to a club or bar in town that had this raised boxing ring at the centre of it. Except there were no ropes around the ring, it was just a large platform. While we were knocking back the booze, a bevy of exotic dancers suddenly appeared on the platform and began dancing provocatively. As we got more and more tipsy, one of the lads suggested to me that I jump on the platform with them as he knew I liked dancing. Fuelled by booze, I paid up the dance fee and shakily climbed up onto the platform to join the girls and started dancing alongside them. All of a sudden, one of the girls gave me a side look and started wailing at the top of her voice while still trying to maintain a musical sound. I was oblivious to the fact that she and her girls were looking at me as if I were a mad man. In fact, I was rather chuffed that they were encouraging, so I played up my dancing with a big silly grin on my face. While I was having the time of my life on stage, I noticed a group of British police officers seated just below me, killing themselves laughing.

Eventually they called me over and said to me, 'Hey lad, do you know what that dancer was singing about?'

I staggered forward to get a better listen. 'No,' I replied, 'what was she saying?'

The copper dissolved into fits of laughter, then choked out, 'Who is this red and hairy fat man?'

In Malaya we had the pleasure of playing for the Gurkhas, the units in the British Army that were made up of Nepalese Gurkha soldiers. They loved us playing marches dressed in white uniform and afterwards were great hosts, feeding us and laying on lots of drink. Now, it might not like seem it, but I'm not actually a big drinker, so it doesn't take long for me to get sloshed. On one of the nights I got so drunk that I got left behind by the rest of my band, who had headed back earlier to our bashas – the local name for the small huts we slept in – a short distance from where we were. Not entirely sure where I was going, I staggered into the night, careful not to slip on the muddy ground that was softer and moister than usual following the recent monsoon. But, of course, as my luck would have it and wearing my lovely crisp, white uniform, I lost my footing and fell face first into a muddy ditch. For a moment, I almost admitted defeat and considered just lying there in the ditch until sun-up. But I knew I'd get a rollicking from our commanding officer, so I reluctantly dragged myself out of the muck and staggered a few more yards along the way before I came across my basha. Desperate for shut-eye, I stripped off and went to sleep. Next morning I awoke a lot brighter than I had expected and was just about to spring out of bed, when memories from the night before flashed into my head. My heart sank as I remembered my drunken plunge into the soggy, wet, muddy ditch, which had left my spotless white uniform looking like it was camouflage. I felt like pulling my sheet over my head and never waking up again. But, instead, I thought I'd better brave it as we had a busy day ahead of us. But when I looked up, I saw my whites hanging there without a spot of mud on them. I had to pinch myself. Had I dreamed my nightmare journey home? Sadly not, as I noticed my face and hands were covered in mud. Then I realised that, while I was asleep, one of the locals assigned to look after our needs must have seen the mucky uniform, taken it away, washed, pressed and starched it and hung it back in place. Whoever had worked their magic on it was a miracle worker.

THE WAR

PART 4

Marrying the girl of my dreams

CHAPTER 14

Family festivities

It makes me feel sad to look back at my early days in Camden. I had fun, for sure, but in retrospect, I can see what I was missing. A happy family life. Don't get me wrong, I loved Father very much. When I joined the Army he would write to me on a regular basis or we would meet up from time to time to have man-to-man chats. As we both got older, I felt our relationship grow stronger by the day and – dare I say it – I saw Father gradually become a happier man as he finally put the difficulties of his marriage behind him.

The sad thing is, all that time I was growing up with my parents, I was unaware that relationships and family life *could* be different. As far as I was concerned, what I was experiencing was typical. It was only when I was embraced so warmly by Joan's nearest and dearest that I realised what being part of a family was supposed to be like. It really was something of an eye-opener to see the togetherness, the camaraderie they all shared. It was alien to me to start with, but the more I saw it, the more I wanted it for myself. They lived happily alongside each other and I can scarcely remember a time when any of them raised their voice to one another. Mam and Dad, as I was encouraged to call them, were what you'd call the ideal couple. Respectful, caring and the perfect family figureheads.

The dynamic between Alice and Norman was just right. Dad, because of his arm, was restricted to what he could do, so Mam did everything around the house, and that worked perfectly for them. She happily kept her family of eight going and would do anything for them.

After that initiation lunch with the family, I pretty much became a regular member of the household as my relationship with Joan grew stronger. Because I was allowed off camp every day, I would spend as much time as I could with Joan, up at the house or out and about in the nearby fields or local pubs. Every week, we continued to go dancing. We never seemed to tire of it, it was what we liked doing most, so why not? My only bugbear was that because of my lack of funds, due to that blasted army mix-up I mentioned earlier, I didn't have much money to buy civilian clothes of my own, so was forced to wear my uniform whenever I met Joan. Luckily for me, with her penchant for men in a uniform, that was never really a problem.

However, her family was aware of my financial predicament and would craftily try to help me out without denting my pride. Sometimes after Sunday lunch, we would sit down as a family for a good-natured game of cards with Joan's maternal grandfather, Grandda Baccy, who also lived in the house. I can't for the life of me remember his real name, but he was referred to as Baccy as he was never seen without his pungent pipe in his hand or in his mouth. Funny how a nickname can stick your head, isn't it? Baccy was a massive character and he was a physically big fella too – he had been a blacksmith at one time in his life and had come to live with the family when his wife died.

Now, I will be the first to say that when it comes to playing cards, I'm down there with the worst. I was certainly no card shark and, to be honest, I neither liked nor understood many card games. But all that changed when I started *winning*. To start with, I thought it was beginner's luck, but then I would win week after week and scoop up the few shillings that were up for grabs each time. Eventually the penny dropped – I didn't actually have luck on my side. I wasn't suddenly very skilled at cards. I had my dear new family to thank for my good fortune. Although I was quietly embarrassed by their attempts to pad out my wallet, I was extremely touched and graciously accepted their kind gesture without letting on I knew what they were up to, and I would whisk Joan off to see the latest Hollywood romantic comedy at the pictures with my winnings.

I was very lucky to have the support of the family. It was funny to think that, at one point, Joan and I had skulked around in the shadows so that her dad wouldn't discover our relationship. And now the same man was asking me along to his club to chew the fat over drinks. I really didn't expect any of it.

This particular year I got to enjoy my first proper family Christmas, which helped me feel like I belonged somewhere. When I was a kid, we never seemed to celebrate the festive period. At least, I can't remember doing so. There was no money to start with. I don't recall putting up any decorations and sometimes Mother and Father weren't even around. However, I do have memories of a Christmas party for kids that was hosted by Father's regiment, which my siblings and I would attend. There was food and singing but, best of all, every child in attendance would be handed a present.

It all felt very posh as we just weren't used to receiving new toys. One year, I recall, I was given a tin fire engine which, for me, was akin to receiving a bar of gold. I was thrilled with the toy and ran its wheels over all the tables and walls at the party, making all the irritating noises a fire engine would make. My unadulterated joy was short-lived, however, when I somehow managed to cut myself deeply on it. Laughter swiftly turned to tears as blood pumped out of the tiny but deep gash on my hand. Father gave me a hanky to wrap around the wound until we got it stitched up. But when I got home, Mother wouldn't let me have stitches, which for some unfathomable reason she had an aversion to, and I was left with an unsightly scar on my hand that you can still see today.

In Durham, however, the locals went to town over the festive period and enjoyed their own unique customs that I found very appealing. You'd have a tree and decorations, an enormous Christmas lunch, and the family would gather around the radio for the King's speech on Christmas Day. The family were all royalists, so this ritual of listening to the monarch addressing the nation was incredibly important to each and every one of us, and especially to Norman and me, who were or had been part of the military and had pledged to fight for king and country.

What I loved about the festive period in the north east is that the local community had their own unusual customs. For one, when younger kids went to bed before midnight on New Year's Eve, they were asked to leave shoes behind the door, so they'd wake up the next morning to find a treat that had been left for them. As the year ended, it was thought of as an old man, like Father Time, and the

New Year was regarded as a child that grew older as the year went on, so all the children would wake up to find their shoes filled with sweets and other treats left by the old year to welcome in the New Year. But the grown-ups had festive traditions of their own, such as one called 'first-footing'. Now, unless you have grown up in the north east, you more than likely have never heard of this. But locals believe that if you welcome a dark-haired stranger into your house after the stroke of midnight on New Year's Eve, good luck will come your way for the next 12 months. Because I was dark-haired and relatively new to the area, Alice asked if I would be her 'first-foot'. Without a moment's hesitation, I happily agreed, even though I didn't know what I was actually letting myself in for.

Alice explained that later that evening she would be hosting a New Year's party and would be inviting a handful of friends, neighbours and family over for an evening of festive revelry.

'And...?' I asked, wondering what my role on the night would involve.

She explained that at five to midnight I would have to leave the party, go to the cree – the shed where the coal was kept, often next to the 'netty' or outside toilet – collect a lump and bring it back to the house after the New Year had been heralded in. I later learned that this was to bring luck, symbolizing that the fire would never go out. In other words, you would have good fortune, warmth and food throughout the year. It all seemed quite straightforward to me, so I didn't think anything of it.

That evening, as we enjoyed a merry time, I did as instructed and threw on an overcoat, retrieved the lump of coal from the shed and waited for the stroke of midnight before knocking on the door. As planned, Alice welcomed me into the house with a peck on the cheek, offered me a slice of cake, a drink and handed me half a crown. Then I threw the lump of coal into the fire, gave each of the ladies in the room a kiss and shook all the fellas' hands. That wasn't hard after all, I thought to myself, as I took a healthy and well-deserved swig of my drink. I was looking forward now to kicking my shoes off and welcoming in the New Year with Joan and the family.

But Norman had other ideas.

'Howay, lad,' he bellowed. 'Up the street, with you. They're all waiting for you.'

I looked at Joan and then back at Norman. I was confused. Who was waiting for me?

Norman explained that he and Alice had informed their neighbours that they would be expecting a 'first-foot' to pay them all a visit. And that 'first-foot' was yours truly.

At first, I thought this was Norman's attempt at New-Year humour, but when he furrowed his brow and made it quite clear that he was deadly serious about my mission, I humbly agreed to take on the task. I kissed a highly amused Joan goodbye, pulled on my winter coat and stepped out into the blustery winter's night.

Every house I visited, I went through the motions of collecting a lump of coal from their cree, knocking on the door and being welcomed in. Then, inside, I'd get a kiss from the women in the house, a handshake from the men, half a crown and, best of all, a drink that most definitely kept me warm as I trundled from one house to the next. I wish I could remember how many homes I visited that night or how many lovely people I met, but I can't. In fact, thanks to the numerous beers and deadly homemade concoctions I swigged, I can't even remember reaching the end of Joan's road. It was all a blank. In fact, Joan's Mam, along with many other women, used to make her own version of a whisky liqueur, a bit like Drambuie, which was highly potent. She also made what she called 'Egg Flip' from sherry and eggs, which was very much like Advocaat.

When I woke up the next morning, I was relieved to find myself in somebody's house. However, when I sat up and opened my weary eyes, I didn't actually know whose house I was in. I tried to remember something from the past few hours, but my last lucid memory was of the first house I visited after I left Joan's. I remember how friendly the family who had welcomed me in was. I just about recall throwing the lump of coal in the fire, but the numerous kisses, the handshakes and the booze were a blur. Then after that, nothing.

Standing, I realised I was barely in a fit state to walk. My head was thumping like my band drum, my legs felt like jelly and my tummy felt like a washing machine. It took all of my strength to stay on two feet and not collapse in a ball and throw up all over the place, wherever I was. All I wanted to do was to get back to Joan's as fast as I could, not only because she must have been frantic with worry that I hadn't made it home, but I also wanted her to pamper me in my fragile state. Shaky on my feet, I stepped quietly out into the landing where I could hear voices coming from downstairs, though I didn't recognize any of them. As I crept as quietly as I could down the stairs, I landed on a step that let out the mightiest of creaks, which caught the attention of the folks in the kitchen.

'Good morning there, lad,' a voice called out. 'Come and join us.' Sheepishly I walked into the kitchen where a delightful family were seated eating their breakfast. They asked me if I wanted to join them for a full English, but the strong smell of grease and oil in the air made me almost double over and chuck up. Luckily I remained strong and passed on their kind offer, asking them instead where I was. I was shocked to discover that my 'first-footing' had taken me as far as the next village, which was some miles away from Oakenshaw. How I got that far is anyone's guess, but it seemed that I had been well looked after by the locals along the way. And that's what I came to discover over time – that village people, especially in mining communities, are such lovely folk who look after each other, even relative strangers, without question.

Perhaps noticing my deathly white pallor, the father of the house hastily offered to take me back to Joan's in his truck. When I finally got home, I was surprised and a little disappointed to discover that my absence hadn't been a cause for concern for the family, not even Joan, whom I had expected to have been at her wits' end. Instead they all found the whole idea of me waking up in a strange house absolutely hilarious. After a wash and a shave and some booze-flavoured kisses, I bade farewell to the family and headed back to my camp to sleep off my hangover.

CHAPTER 15

Popping the question

Is it ever too early to think about marriage? Maybe in these modern times it is, as people are faced with so many choices. But, back in the days when I was a kid, getting wed was something that you thought about from the minute you met someone special. In those days, lovers would marry young. Mother was just 16 when she married Father, who was in his mid-twenties, while Alice and Norman got hitched when they were barely out of their teens. So when I say I was seriously considering walking Joan up the aisle, I wasn't mucking about, even though I was only 19 and Joan just 18. Life was really coming together. I had a stable career in the Army, which was a veritable dream come true, I had found the loving support of a family I never expected to find and I had met the girl of my dreams, who had transformed my life beyond recognition. Joan was everything to me, and the more and more time we spent together, the more I realised that I never needed to look at another woman again. It was true. I felt as though after making Joan, God had thrown away the mould. She was the only woman I could ever want, and I wasn't one of those fellas whose head was easily turned. I had got into the habit of telling her that I loved her. We even ended up creating our own language that only we understood, and we dreamed up ridiculous names for each other. I used to call her Plo, while she'd call me Hunk. I was also called Collywobble. The silly things you say to each other when you're in love, eh? And so the idea of marriage spun constantly around in my head. Joan and I had discussed the prospect of becoming Mr and Mrs Thackery on numerous occasions, but we never really talked about it in a serious context.

But two things convinced me that perhaps tying the knot was something we should finally get around to doing.

For one, my beloved Aunty Maisie who, along with my grandparents, had been very good to me at times during my childhood, gave Joan and her family the seal of approval. Aunty Maisie and Nan were the most important family members to me as I was growing up in London when Father was away, so it was important to me that they loved Joan as much as I did. However, when I first mentioned to them that I was seeing a lovely girl, I was concerned because they instantly referred to Joan as 'that girl'. I would later gather that their cool response was simply because they were being protective of me, cautious of any girl who dared to get involved with their golden boy.

However, all that changed when Maisie and her husband Jack met the family. The pair of them were heading up north to see friends so I suggested that they stop off in Oakenshaw to meet Joan and her parents while I was away with my regiment. When they arrived, Alice and Norman showed them such great hospitality and invited Maisie and Jack to stay with them for a short time, which they readily agreed to. During their stay, Joan's mam and dad were incredibly generous to them, tending to their every need. Like me, Maisie was touched by their care and later confided in me that she thought the family 'were lovely people', which was music to my ears.

The other factor that made me consider marriage more seriously was news that the 45th Regiment was being deployed to Korea to assist in the war that had just started raging between China and the US. The order, which came via telegram while I was on leave, left me in two minds. Part of me was exhilarated that this would be my first time heading out to battle as an active soldier. This was what we had been training for all those years and I was excited.

But I also harboured the fear that I'm sure most soldiers must feel when they hear they are being shipped out to war – the fear of not making it back home. When I first signed up to the Army, it was instilled in me that we were fighting for king and country and that in order to uphold all that was good, I must be willing to put my life on the line. But that was before Joan had waltzed into my life. Being in love and enjoying life in the warm bosom of a loving family seriously altered my mindset. However, as much as I wanted to stay home with my beloved, I was a soldier who was committed to defending people who were being done wrong. Besides, back then, as a soldier, you had it ingrained in you that you did what you were told.

Breaking the news to Joan about Korea was one of the toughest things I ever had to do. As soon as the words came out of my mouth, I could see her shoulders droop slightly and tears well in her eyes. Neither of us wanted this to happen and we both agreed that it felt like a cruel twist of fate that, just as we had found each other, we were being ripped apart. I tried to make things better by assuring her that our involvement in the war probably wouldn't last all that long and that more than likely I would be home again by Christmas. But I could see that she wasn't convinced. I think she was more concerned about losing the man she had fallen in love with. I was scared about that too – who wouldn't be? – but I could never let her see that side of me. Instead, I promised her that I would be home before she knew it, no matter what. To give her credit, she understood that people did as they were told in the Army, that there was no point in arguing and that you just bloody well got on with it.

I suggested that we finally put our money where our mouths were and get married as soon as possible so that our strong bond was made even stronger than it already was. And so I uttered the words I had been dying to utter for months – 'Joan, will you marry me?' Joan smiled through her tears and kissed me repeatedly, wrapping her arms around me as tightly as she could, whispering, 'Yes, yes, yes,' in my ear. In retrospect, perhaps I am a little disappointed that my proposal wasn't as elaborate as the ones you see online these days, but I meant every word. All I wanted was to spend my every day with this wonderful, beautiful young woman. I just prayed I'd make it home again in one piece.

CHAPTER 16

Wedding preparations

I've always been a traditional kind of fella so, once I'd popped the question, I knew I had another important mission to undertake – to formally ask Norman for his daughter's hand in marriage. This is possibly one of the most nerve-wracking moments in a man's life as fathers-in-law invariably tend to be very protective of their daughters. But I didn't actually feel too nervous about approaching Norman because we had developed a strong friendship and would meet up on a regular basis. We would talk about every subject under the sun, although the conversations would end up with Norman sharing his war stories. The battle tales he'd tell me were brutal and harsh without any fancy flourish. This was in stark contrast to the memories he'd share at home, which were much more light-hearted. I guess as a dad, he didn't want his family to know how hard life on the front-line had actually been for him. They had, of course, seen the harsh consequences of war when he returned home from the Somme without an arm, but some of the things Norman had experienced during the First World War, such as its stark brutality and the tragic death of friends, were far more terrifying than anyone could imagine and certainly he felt were not appropriate for the delicate ears of his wife and daughters.

I arranged to meet Norman at the bar, telling him I had a question to ask of him. I think he knew what I was planning to tell him but he didn't say anything. We'd spoken about marriage before and I was confident that he would not stand in the way of our plans.

He knew me very well now and all those initial qualms he'd had about me being a fly-by-night soldier were long gone. In fact, I think he had already started to see me as another son, so getting married to Joan would merely be a case of going through the motions to make it legal. And that made me very happy indeed.

Bizarrely, as I approached the club for our rendezvous, I was filled with nerves as the whole idea of marriage suddenly seemed so big. Ordering a round of drinks, I told Norman straight, 'Dad, we want to get married.' I waited for a reaction, but there was none to start with. Instead, he looked deep in thought. The hesitation worried me. This wasn't the reaction I had anticipated. Then he let a smile grip his lips, wrapped an arm around my shoulders and gave me one of those London hugs he had been so curious about when I had first came to lunch. 'Colin,' he finally broke the silence, 'you're already like a son to me, and I can see how happy you make my daughter, so I would be happy for you and Joan to get married. But let me ask you something...'

I hesitated. Dad looked serious.

'With this business in Korea,' he began, 'is it a good idea to do it now? Do you not think it might be best to wait and see if...'

He didn't need to finish what he was about to say. I knew where he was going with it. And he was right. I might not come back from the war and where would that leave poor Joan?

'That's exactly why we should do it now,' I replied. 'I want to experience the joy of marriage with a woman I love. Just like you and Alice have for many years.'

Norman took in what I said and nodded his approval.

'Well, I guess I'm hardly one to talk, am I?' he laughed, holding up his glistening hook hand. 'I did the same thing before the First World War and look at Alice and me now. I guess nothing has changed, except these days it damn well hurts if I scratch my head!'

I chuckled. 'I love your daughter very much, Norman,' I said. 'I would do anything for her. I know there is a chance I might not come home from Korea, but if I don't get the chance to marry the girl of my dreams, I will feel like I will have missed out on the greatest thing to ever happen to me. Joan is well aware of the risks, and she says she loves me and that she's willing to wait for me. Dad, I promise, I will come home again and then Joan and I can start a family and enjoy a happy life.'

I could tell that my heartfelt words were getting to Dad.

'Do I have your blessing?'

Norman looked like he was almost on the verge of shedding a tear. But I stress the word 'almost'. Dad wasn't the type to shed a tear. Instead, he remained stoic and suddenly got to his feet as if a commanding officer had just walked into the room.

'Of course you have, son,' he declared, extending his hook to shake. We both laughed and fell into a very manly hug.

News of our impending marriage went down a storm with the family and Alice couldn't wait to get started on the preparations for the big day, already having enlisted the services of her daughters to help out and giving each of them a specific role to focus on.

The girls were always willing to help out the family. Dad had already roped them in to helping out at the club, which they did happily. However, while they had no problems wiping down the bar, cleaning the floors or picking up the rubbish, the only task they despised was cleaning the urinals. Joan, in particular, hated that task. 'I can't bear the smell,' she'd always moan. And yet they still did it because it was helping their dad out.

Alice wasn't just a perfect housewife, she was also a dab hand at organizing big events like weddings. I already knew she was a phenomenal cook, but Alice had quietly carved out a successful sideline planning and catering for wedding parties in the area. Not only would she prepare the most tasty food and dream up the delicious ingredients for the centrepiece wedding cake, she would also arrange the reception at Dad's club, which is how the club made a lot of its money. Unsurprisingly, the word of mouth was really quite extraordinary, so everyone in the local area knew exactly where to go if they wanted their day to go with a bang and for their guests to go home with their taste buds begging for more.

At Easter, Alice and her girls would come up with the most beautiful and intricately designed dyed eggs for the local Easter egg hunts. They had the process of creating them down to a tee. They would wrap the eggs in fern leaves and muslin, and many other things besides, and boil them in the dye until they went hard. Then, once the eggs had cooled, they'd peel off the muslin and leaves to reveal a beautiful pattern. Some were so intricate that you'd have thought a skilled and celebrated artist was responsible. But it was just Alice. Her dyed eggs also went down a storm with the locals and she would often pick up a money prize at the annual competitions at the local clubs. Easter was called Paste or Pace Egg day locally. They had names for all the Sundays leading up to Easter and children used to recite them as a skipping or 'two-ball' rhyme, singing 'Tid, Mid, Miseray, Carlin, Palm, Pace Egg Day'.

Alice had, over the years, built up a rather fierce reputation that had some folks in awe of her skills. To say Alice was competitive was an understatement. She threw herself into what she did but always with an eye on the prize. However, her eagerness to win and her natural talent at cooking didn't always work in her favour. For years, she had been a keen member of the Women's Institute. But after winning prizes year after year, she was taken to one side and asked to take a step back from entering the contests because some of the other green-eyed members of the WI were seething into their cooking bowls. She was put out to start with, as all she was doing was what she loved best, but years later she was able to look back with a laugh about how she had ruffled the feathers of all those women.

The date we chose for the big day was 20 September, which was about two weeks or so before I was due to head out to Korea. All of a sudden, the wedding preparations kicked into gear and Joan's sisters were dashing around the place, trying to get things in order. I volunteered my services, but Alice and the girls wouldn't have it. You see, the women were in charge of weddings and the fellas weren't required – unless something needed lifting, of course. Otherwise the men would be thrown out. 'Men,' the girls told us, time and time again, 'just get in the way.' Up in Durham, the women were the strong ones who took control of things like that, and that was that. No arguments! And who were we to argue with that?

This situation may sound a little outdated in our progressive world of today, but that's just the way it was back then. It was a time when men went to work while women looked after the household. Men weren't allowed to see their children being born like they are today (which is still one of my life's regrets) and you would never see a fella dare to push a pram in the street – that was seen then as a woman's job. Of course, the world is different now and I am happy to see that marriages are more about equality and that men get stuck in as much as women.

The night before the wedding my father came up to meet the family. Like Maisie, he took to them brilliantly. He loved Joan and could see exactly why I was so in love with her. I was pleased that he did. Part of me thinks he was in awe of what Joan and I had, because you could see from a mile off that our relationship was full of love and that we had a unique bond and such heartfelt respect for each other. Looking back, I wonder if he ever looked at the two of us and wished that his marriage to my mother had been like that.

I was also pleased that Father really got on with Norman. That really made my day. It was important for me that they both bonded. Norman was a second father to me and I was lucky to have him.

The night before the wedding was a relatively calm one. Joan and I decided to uphold tradition and spend our final night apart. She stayed at home while I stayed with her brother Henry, whom I had asked to be best man, and his wife Joyce. There was no stag do, they weren't really a thing back then, so we popped instead to the local pub for a few drinks. But not too many, mind. I was determined to remember the next day in vivid clarity because that was the memory I wanted to take away with me to Korea to keep me strong for however long we were out there.

That night I went to bed full of excitement. Nerves didn't bother me. I just couldn't wait for the morning to come around so that I could finally marry my Joan.

CHAPTER 17

Getting wed
and shipping out

It was a bright, sunny day when Henry, Father and I walked down the hill towards St Stephen's in Willington. The church was small, but impressive to the eye with its mighty tower looming high above the churchyard. It had stood in the village for as long as anyone could remember and, though it was actually built in 1857, it was believed that the tower dated back to medieval times.

Inside, the church was smaller than it looked from the outside. Rows of pews filled the main hall and at the top of the aisle was an arch that led to the altar. Guests were already piling in to get the best seats and I was surprised to see so many people as I strolled down the aisle decked out in my battledress. To be honest, I recognized very few faces as they were mainly from Joan's side of the family. Only my father represented me. Mother was estranged from the family and my siblings, Shirley, Maisie, Mike and Brian were living with a foster parent, Mrs Pilbeam in Hastings.

When the wedding march sounded, I felt butterflies in my stomach as I anticipated Joan's arrival. I could hear people turning in the aisles to catch their first glimpse of the glowing bride, but I chose to wait until her dad deposited her by my side before I took her all in.

When I sensed that she had arrived beside me, I turned to look at her and was totally in awe. I already knew that Joan was a gorgeous girl, but decked out in her pink suit, matching hat and immaculately made-up face, she simply blew me away. She had never looked as beautiful.

Joan wore the pink suit because white wedding gowns were expensive back then. Still are, as it turns out – especially bearing in mind they are worn for just a day. It's bonkers!

The ceremony was pretty straightforward, but it felt emotional for Joan and me because we knew that this special day was all we were going to have to remember for quite some time, what with me heading off to Korea in a fortnight or so. When we recited the vows, we listened to every word and meant every single one as we repeated them. And when we kissed, we made it last for as long as was appropriate.

After the ceremony, we headed off to Dad's club in the village for the reception. I was too shy – or was that too choked up? – at the time to do a speech, but I think Father did – all I remember is everyone laughing. Norman said a few words about how I was a great addition to the family, which meant the world to me. After the wedding breakfast, we took to the floor for our first dance. I cannot for the life of me remember what the song was but, as you can imagine, Joan and I put on a good show, looking each other in the eye for the duration, just as we had when we met that first time on the dance floor over a year ago.

Our honeymoon was at Mam's house – it was all we could afford as we had no money for any trips. But that was fine with us. With my impending departure, all I wanted to do was spend as much time with Joan before I had to say goodbye.

In truth, marriage didn't change anything. I didn't feel any different. I didn't love Joan any more than I already did. I still felt like the same chap I had the day before. I guess, because Joan and I had been so inseparable all that year, we'd already felt like a married couple.

What I did feel was that I finally had someone to look after me and give me the support I had always needed – not that I required mollycoddling. But little did I know that having Joan in my life would be the best thing that ever happened to me. She truly became the wind beneath my wings, guiding me through both good times and bad times and encouraging me to try my hardest so that I could achieve everything I put my mind to.

The days leading up to my departure to Korea were like a ticking time bomb and went way too fast for my liking. I was oblivious to the rest of the world, all I wanted to do was be with Joan. And we were inseparable. The family organized a farewell meal, which was nice, and Mam and Dad offered beautiful words about how special I was to them and their daughter. The words touched me deeply. Our last night together was just terrible. I wanted to go back to the barracks and tell them I wasn't going. I wasn't ready to leave my wife just yet. I didn't want to be apart for any length of time. The commanding officer at the barracks hadn't given us too much information about how long we'd be away, but only to expect the unexpected. I stayed awake most of that last night cradling a sobbing Joan in my arms. I wanted to remember as much of our last moments together before

I left. I must have fallen asleep eventually because the next morning Joan was up and already dressed when she nudged me awake.

The 45th had moved down to a barracks in Colchester a few weeks back, so the plan was for the family to take me to Durham station where we would say our final goodbyes. Henry drove us all there and everyone piled out. Mam, Dad and Henry wished me luck and told me they looked forward to seeing me again soon and then hung back while Joan accompanied me to the platform. There, we simply looked at each other, not saying a word but communicating in our own way. 'I will see you soon,' I said eventually. 'Think of me every day and I will think of you.' 'Always,' was Joan's response, trying to stifle her tears. Suddenly, the guard blew his whistle and we both knew that this was it – it was time for me to leave and we had to say our final goodbyes. I closed my eyes and kissed her gently, savouring it for as long as I could. I wanted to remember this special kiss when I was thousands of miles away, surrounded by other soldiers putting their lives at risk. I told myself that whenever I was feeling down or scared or felt like giving up, I would think about this beautiful kiss and remember what was waiting for me back home.

Reluctantly, I broke the embrace, snatched up my bag and told Joan I loved her one last time. I hopped on the train, dashing to a window just as the train's engine fired up. As it started to chug its way out of the station, my heart ached as the image of a tearful Joan, now surrounded by her family, faded rapidly into the distance before disappearing completely in clouds of smoke.

After changing at London, destined for Colchester, I must have fallen asleep shortly after because the next thing I knew I was at

Colchester station where the whole regiment was gathered waiting for the train to take us on to Southampton where we would board the ship to Korea. It was good to see the lads again. I'd been so caught up with Joan and our wedding plans that I hadn't really given them a second thought. Second in command, Major Withers was there in his military finest, barking orders and keeping us all in line. However, he had a surprise in store for us. The major was the brother of the famous and very beautiful actress Googie Withers and, as a treat, he had brought her along to say farewell to all the boys.

Needless to say, the fellas were all of a dither at the prospect of breathing in the same air as a bona fide superstar. It was all anyone could talk about, which I guess was a clever way of distracting the boys from heading off to war and the terrifying times we had ahead.

When she finally appeared, the boys started howling like wolves baying at the moon, some climbing over each other to get a better look at her. She really did look amazing, everything you would expect a screen starlet to look like with that magical glow that stars have. Even though the lads sounded like animals in a zoo, Googie seemed to lap up the attention and blew them all kisses.

Suddenly, Major Withers bellowed, 'Thackery – sound the mount', which was an old trumpet call. Dutifully I did as I was told and the troops automatically piled onto the train, looking over their shoulders to get one last glimpse of Googie. Within seconds of everyone climbing aboard, the windows along the train were pulled down and about a hundred heads popped out trying to get a final peek at the superstar and also to seek out those family members who had accompanied them to the station. While they were looking out, Googie surprised me by planting a big kiss on my cheek, which caused the fellas to launch into a bout of enthusiastic cheering and wolf-whistling. Red faced, I joined the others on the train and settled back in my seat as it pulled out of the station towards Southampton, and I wondered what I could expect when we arrived in Korea in around six weeks.

Oddly, I felt no nerves. I wasn't at all scared about going to war. In fact, I was more curious. This was what I had trained for all these years – to be a soldier – and I wanted to know how it felt to be in combat after all the practice we had done. I was sure nothing could compare to the reality of warfare, the thunderous sound of gunshots and explosions, the uncertainty of what to expect and the bone-chilling fear of being wounded or killed. But our training had prepared us for this and now, finally, I was heading out into the world to experience war for the first time. Was I ready? I had to be. And yet it felt just like yesterday when I first stepped into an army barracks.

PART 5

The Korean War

CHAPTER 18

Realities of war

As the ship set sail to Korea, all I could think about was my darling Joan left behind, just days after we had become husband and wife. It felt cruel to just up and leave the way I did. I knew that she understood why I had to go. That it was an order from on high. I guess I could have backed out, but I had trained for years to serve my country and this was my opportunity to do it.

The truth of the matter was that I wasn't entirely sure what we were actually fighting for. I knew we were going to a place called Korea, although I had no idea where that was, and that we were supporting the US troops, but that was pretty much it. It was only later that I would understand the history of the conflict.

The geo-political events that had led up to the conflict were complex. After the Second World War, the US and Soviet Union, who had been allies against Nazi Germany, began a fight for power and influence across Europe, with the Soviets intent on spreading communism across Eastern Europe in countries such as Poland, Hungary, Romania, Czechoslovakia and what would become East Germany. A 'cold war' ensued and, to prevent the Soviet Union's influence gaining ground across Europe, the US employed what was known as a policy of containment in countries in the west, such as France, Italy and Greece, and pledged to give financial help to European countries that might be suffering instability, in case such weakness opened the door to a communist takeover.

Berlin had been divided at the end of the Second World War and, in 1948, France, Britain and the US began to unite their zones in West Berlin. Furious, the Soviets cut off the Western Allies' passage into the city, meaning no supplies could be delivered to the areas controlled by the Allies. In response, Britain and the US airlifted supplies into West Berlin until the blockade was called off, 213 days later. Berlin escalated tensions between 'West' and 'East' political factions across the globe.

Twelve nations (the US, Belgium, Canada, Denmark, France, Iceland, Italy, Luxembourg, the Netherlands, Norway, Portugal and the UK) formed the North Atlantic Treaty Organization (NATO) in 1949. This move angered the Soviet Union, who went on to create an alliance with the communist governments of Eastern Europe, known as the Warsaw Pact, in 1955.

Korea had been annexed by the Japanese in 1910 but, following Japan's defeat in the Second World War, the US and the Soviets divided up Korea as they had with Berlin, with the communist country occupying the northern part while their western rivals took on the south. The UN tried to hold elections in Korea, with the aim of resolving the division, but the Soviet Union disagreed and elections were held only in the south. The Soviet Union instead established a Communist Republic under the leadership of Kim Il-sung, known as the Democratic People's Republic of Korea (DPRK). The US, in turn, created the Republic of Korea

(ROK) in the south, under the leadership of the head of the former Provisional Government, Syngman Rhee. Both sides claimed the legitimate right to the whole of Korea; neither believed the border would be permanent.

On 25 June 1950, the North Korean Communist Army, backed by the Soviets, crossed the 38th Parallel and invaded South Korea. Communist China then waded in to help North Korea. Worried that the invasion posed a threat to national interests, the US and Britain pleaded with the UN to let them retaliate. While the US kicked into action days after the invasion, the British Army would be called into the fray a couple of months later. The UN Command was formed of 21 countries, but 90 per cent of the troops were American. The decision was a controversial one for the British Labour Government of the time because the conflict didn't appear to pose a threat to the country's interests. However, with US encouragement, Britain decided to get involved, which is how I ended up on a boat to Korea.

The idea of entering into an international conflict excited me a little. I was actually going to war; I was heading out to help defend a country under attack and uphold what was right. At the same time, I was nervous. Who knew what lay ahead? How long would the battle rage? Could this trigger the start of a third world war, so soon after the last war? Would I make it back in one piece? Would I make it back at all? That's the question that haunted me most. After having only just found my darling Joan, was I about to lose her? And what about Joan? She was the one having to stay at home, not knowing what was going on all those miles away, not knowing if I were alive or dead. We promised to write to each other every week, but how long would it take a letter to travel from Britain to Korea anyway? And what guarantee was there that I'd receive it?

The journey was going to take six weeks and I could have quite easily tortured myself with these questions and more for the duration, but luckily some bright spark called Major Andrews came up with the idea for a ship's concert party and was looking for volunteers. My Brancepeth mates, Sefton and Ken, and I didn't waste any time whatsoever and signed up. The group started rehearsing straightaway and it was a lot of fun coming up with ideas for shows. Luckily, it took up a lot of our time, so we were never bored during the long voyage.

Like on any long journey, the ship would stop off at various ports to pick up supplies and, as usual, troops were allowed some shore leave, where drunken adventures would predictably take place. When we docked at Colombo, I hit the bars with two mates. As we set off in search of a watering hole, one of them said to me, 'While we're here, let's get you a tattoo like us.' Rolling up his sleeve, he exposed a muscled arm covered in some kind of elaborate body art.

'No way,' I hit back, squirming at his design. 'There's no way I'm gonna have one of them!'

We carried on along the way, thinking nothing of it, but I should have known better because, unbeknown to me, they had already hatched a plan.

After a couple of hours of bar hopping, the three of us were legless. What I wasn't aware of was that they were slipping me larger measures than they were drinking, which meant that I was getting drunker much faster. In the last bar we were in, as I got up off my stool, my legs collapsed beneath me and I hit the floor. Gallantly, my two mates heaved me up, wrapped my arms around their necks and dragged me along the street back to the ship. By this point I was apparently pretty much comatose and didn't know what was going on. My two mates then pulled me into a tattoo parlour and asked the tattoo artist to give me a tattoo. They chose a design with hearts, flowers and arrows going through the heart and they suggested that he add, 'Joan, forever yours'.

As he started to ink my arm, I was dimly aware of the incessant whir of a machine and a tickly sensation on my skin. All of a sudden, I was awake, and my first reaction was to thwack the fella out of the way. I looked at my arm – the tattooist had already etched J-O-A-N into my skin – and I pushed the guy aside, knocking all his equipment all over the floor. Looking back, I feel really bad about my reaction because he was actually the innocent victim in all this. I should have taken it out on my two mates instead.

Terrified, the poor tattoo artist started calling out for the military police. 'Fellas,' I said to my two mates. 'Run, I'll see you back at the ship.' It was a joke gone wrong and there was no need for all three of us to get in trouble, so I thought I'd just take it on the chin on my own.

Moments after they left, the military police burst in and restrained me. The tattoo artist explained that I had hit him and smashed the place up. I held my hands up and took the blame. After all, that was what had happened. Kind of. Keen to resolve the issue, the military police asked if I had any money to cover the damage. They searched me and handed the tattooist all the money that they found on me.

Then they cuffed me, bundled me into a jeep and took me back to the ship where I was put under arrest and thrown into the brig, in the depths of the vessel. The next morning, I awoke with a killer hangover and the news that I had been sentenced to three days in the ship's prison cells. For the next 36 hours, I endured the most punishing three days of boredom imaginable and couldn't wait to be set free.

When the ship reached the tropics, the troops had a habit of sleeping up on deck, either on the ground or in a hammock. One night, I was on night picket duty, ensuring everyone was safe, when all of a sudden I got the fright of my life. Across the deck from me I could see this white thing that looked as if it was glowing, slap -bang in the middle of some of the other troops. From where I was standing I couldn't quite make it out, but as I drew nearer I saw that it was a man – but an incredibly white one with his eyes wide open. My colleague said to me, 'Is he dead?' and I replied, 'I'm not sure. Let me check.' I nudged the chap with the tip of my toe and, all of a sudden, this huge white fella (probably an albino) jumped up in the air, told me to sod off, and lay back down and went straight back to sleep. I've never seen someone so ghostly pale and I never saw that soldier again.

When we arrived in Pusan, we had to stay on the ship while everything was made ready for us to disembark. As we waited on the deck, we had a grand old time listening to an amazing American army band on the quayside, who had come to greet us. They were performing some fabulous songs, including 'St Louis Blues', whilst marching up and down the quay. It was only after a while that we noticed they were a segregated band as they were all black (the US Army didn't fully end racial segregation in their armed forces until after the end of the Korean War in 1953). We'd never seen anything like that before. They were superb musicians.

Once we had disembarked, all the troops then boarded a train that was taking us north to Suwon and field rations were distributed. The journey took a lot longer than expected because the train had to keep stopping as the infrastructure was so damaged after six months of war. But at least the regular stops enabled us to make meals by the side of the tracks and to get hot water from the steam engine pulling the train. Thus, a journey that was not much further than London to Scotland took five days. It was freezing outside too. Most people don't realise how extreme the Korean climate is – it's roasting in summer and freezing in winter. The countryside was bleak – ravaged by war – and the weather was dismal.

When we got to our base in Suwon, we discovered to our surprise that there were no vehicles or guns waiting for us. It was then explained to us that the equipment was coming on a later ship. We couldn't believe that they had sent the men before the equipment – it really made us laugh.

The commanding officers wanted us to be occupied so kept us on alert. At this time, refugees were coming over the border thick and fast, escaping the communist regime in North Korea. Some of them were enemy infiltrators who would come at us, given half a chance. They were clever blighters, mind, because they had women with them and they knew we wouldn't shoot at women – some of them would even dress as women to fool us. So we ended up chasing these people up into the hills. We all felt sympathy for the plight of the poor genuine refugees, some of whom were in a really terrible state, fleeing south, away from the fighting. The British soldiers often shared their rations with the near-starving flood of people moving south.

I remember the first time I ever got shot at. While our artillery guns had not yet arrived, we did have road vehicles, including Bren Gun carriers, which are like small tanks that the infantry use. I was operating this wireless set behind a steel plate and, all of sudden, I could hear this 'bang, bang, bang'. I started. 'What was that?' Someone said, 'Get your head down, you silly bugger, you're being shot at.' So I ducked very quickly. The infiltrators were firing at us from a hilltop and I could barely make them out. In that moment, life suddenly became much more serious – this was not an exercise!

During those weeks we spent a lot of time on foot, chasing the infiltrators and killing as many of them as we could. At this point, we were housed in the ruins of an old school building. Because we were being targeted, I had no qualms about retaliating. It was kill or be killed. That's what we had been trained to do. I discovered that once you have been shot at, it sort of wakes something up in your mind and you find it easier to shoot back.

Some of us did get shot and injured, but luckily no one was killed. If one of the boys got shot, they were immediately taken to the regimental aid post. If you took a prisoner and he was injured, you would also take him to the same place. You see, the British Army will never ill-treat prisoners who have surrendered or been captured.

They would have their arms taken off them, be strip-searched and left with anything personal such as photographs. Then they would be taken to the nearest cookhouse where they got fed – they would be well looked after.

Eventually, the guns arrived and we went to meet the train to bring all the equipment back to our temporary base. We formed into a regiment before moving up into the line to do what we were there to do. In the brigade, there were three battalions of infantry – the Royal Ulster Rifles, the Northumberland Fusiliers and the Gloucestershire Regiment, commonly referred to as the Glorious Glosters. We had three batteries of guns in the regiment, each responsible for supporting a battalion of infantrymen by firing on the enemy before and during the initial stages of an advance. My battery was called 70 Battery and we supported the Glosters. My role was assistant to the observation post officer, whose job was to direct the firing – if he got killed, I would have to take over, so effectively we had the same role. We would advance with the infantry in support of them. Our orders came from the company commander, who would tell our officers the plan of action, which would then be fed back to us.

The first attack I was involved in was Hill 327 in February 1951 as part of a counter-offensive following UN forces retreat from the Battle of the Ch'ongch'on River the previous December. The Chinese had control of it and were heavily entrenched there, so the idea was to push them back. The Americans had a habit of chucking napalm bombs at them. The smell was awful, like burnt pork. And the screams – the screams were just terrible. But in this instance we were to attack without air support and, prior to the infanty attack, the enemy positions were to be shelled by our artillery guns and tanks. As assistant to the officer responsible for ordering artillery fire on the enemy, my job was to advance forward with him with a wireless operator. I would carry the set, enabling him to operate it on my back, while he carried the batteries. Both the officer and I would carry a map, compass and board to write observations and calculations on. That way, if the officer became a casualty, I could take over with my duplicate equipment.

I was with a chap called Paddy Drumm, who was the wireless operator, and Captain A M L Newcombe MC RA (who was affectionately known as Recce Newcombe, I assume due to his skills of reconnaissance). The three of us had moved forward from a position some way behind the front-line. When we got there, Paddy and I stopped, while Captain Newcombe went off into the pitch-black night to find the company commander. We were standing there waiting, but we knew something was about to happen, we knew the bombardment was about to start. We really couldn't see anything around us. Then, all of a sudden, a massive flash lit up the night, followed by one heck of a noise. Paddy and I hit the ground, thrown off our feet. We were unsure what had just happened but, as we gradually regained our composure, we realised we were under the muzzle of a British twenty-pounder Centurion tank that was firing into the mountain – and we'd got the full blast of it. For a good while, Paddy and I could hear nothing but ringing, and I swear that incident is partly, if not totally, responsible for the fact that I wear two hearing aids today!

Shortly afterwards, the three of us were ordered forwards with the infantry company we were there to support. We advanced, firing at the enemy positions on the hill above us, with the enemy returning fire. It took some time to clear the hill and reach the top, with the blast of the tank gun still ringing in my ears. By then, the enemy had fled their hilltop positions and things quietened down. It was still the middle of the night. Our routine was to observe from our position and report back anything unusual on the radio. Recce and I shared the night-time watch duty – I slept first and relieved him later in the night. I crawled into the observation trench previously manned by the enemy. I wore a headset attached to a long lead, snaking out to the radio some distance away, and observed the surrounding terrain as best I could in the circumstances – this was, of course, many years before night-vision binoculars were invented. It was extremely cold at night. You had to keep moving otherwise you were in danger of getting a severe case of frostbite. The temperatures were so low; sometimes the wind-chill was minus 40 and I did actually get frostbite. I never knew I had it at the time, but it is something that has led to continuing problems my entire life.

At first light, a chap called Busty Greenhalgh crept up the hill armed with some piping-hot tea. We chatted for a moment, then he asked me, 'Who's your friend?'

'What friend?' I replied.

Busty gestured behind me. I followed the line of his pointed finger and, to my horror, discovered that I'd been sitting all night up against a dead Chinese soldier, with his face no more than six inches from me. It was one heck of a shock!

We stayed on the hilltop for a few days before being relieved, then returned to the battery position a few miles back from the front-line.

Some time later we were in the process of relieving an observation party after an attack on another hill, waiting by a road with a large group of infantrymen. While orderlies filled ambulances with casualties from prior assaults, a medical sergeant suddenly started roaring at the driver to get out of his seat and start helping to transport the injured into the back of his van. The driver appeared not to hear the order being barked at him. Instead, once the ambulance was filled to capacity, the driver immediately drove off and headed back to the aid station. A while later he returned, the ambulance empty and ready to collect more injured men. Once again, the sergeant demanded that the driver get out of the vehicle and help transport stretchers, but still the fella refused to move. Furious that the driver still appeared to be disobeying an order, the sergeant stormed over to the ambulance and yanked open the door to discover the driver sitting in a pool of his own blood. It turned out that the driver had been shot, but was so determined to get the injured soldiers back to the hospital, he'd kept driving in spite of the pain he was in. What a hero! I never found out what happened to the driver, but I sincerely hope he got a medal for his valiant actions.

We were, at times, required to support troops from other nations. On one particular day we were travelling through a village with an allied infantry regiment from another nation. Up ahead, we could hear the pained screams and wails of a man in agony. It was a horrid, torturous sound. We knew something wasn't right, so my captain ordered me to go forward to see what was going on. As I got close, a terrible scene met my eyes. Two soldiers stood on either side of a young Chinese man pinned to a chair. The soldiers were feverishly smashing their rifle butts against his knees. Every thwack was agony to him and the poor fella was howling like a wounded dog. As I got nearer, I could see that the unfortunate victim had already been shot in the knee, so his beating was only making his agony worse. I shouted at the soldiers and pulled out my pistol. Shocked, the two soldiers jumped aside. I ordered them to get away from the terrorized man, telling them the Chinese soldier was now a prisoner of the British Army. I placed his arm around my shoulders and, leaning my body against his injured leg to act as a crutch, I walked him back to our vehicle.

Suddenly, he uttered a few words – in perfect English!

'Thank you so much. It's lovely to be in British hands.'

We talked further and it turned out he had been studying at university when he had been reluctantly recruited into the Army and he didn't have any interest in fighting.

We took him back to headquarters, where he was questioned by officers to see what they could get out of him. I should add that he was never ill-treated. The British don't beat prisoners; they are questioned, of course, but they are treated well. I was always told that by treating prisoners well, we would get more out of them anyway.

Later on, the student gave me a silver coin called a Maria Theresa Thaler, which was as large as a half crown and named after the Habsburg empress from the 18th century. I was very touched by his gesture as I had only been doing my job, but I could see he was a good man and I was glad I had been there to help when he needed it. I never saw him again, but I held on to the coin for a while – until, that is, our jeep almost toppled over a pontoon bridge that stretched out over a river and sent our kit, which had been tied loosely to the roof, crashing into the Han River. I'm gutted I lost that coin and, to this day, I still wonder whatever happened to that poor lad.

The war threw up some terrible sights. Bodies were lying on the ground everywhere you went and there were lots of injured men needing to be tended to. It was horrific. However, over time we became immune to the dreadful things around us and I got used to seeing death. You began just to walk over or step around the bodies, there were so many about. Fortunately, there wasn't that strong an odour of death because the weather was so cold.

There was one sight that I did find repulsive. We were advancing through another village and stumbled across the trussed-up body of an allied soldier. The villagers told us that he had raped a girl from the village, so they had tied him up and condemned him to a death of a thousand cuts. The body was stinking and there was blood all over the place – all we could do was take note of the grid reference and get someone else to take it away. We never knew who the fella was as he had no dog tags or anything in the way of identification. It was an awful thing to see.

You might think that this demonstrated that relations with the villagers were strained but, in truth, it was the opposite. While we were there, they knew that they were safe and that they wouldn't be ill-treated. We Brits were different to the other nations on patrol. We were very generous to women and children. You'd see our boys open up tins of cheese, biscuits and jam for the locals, who were always very hungry. We'd get tins of boiled sweets in our rations and the kids loved them. Even the roughest of our blokes would soften up quickly as soon as they saw kids. It was something quite amazing. I think it was the way we were brought up and it's a part of the British character of which I'm particularly proud.

The only way Joan and I kept in touch in 1950, whilst I was in Korea, was by letter – our world then was very unlike that of today, with our reliance on mobile phones! Mail was very important to a soldier away from home – you only had to witness a chap's reaction when everyone else got a letter and he didn't, sometimes only because a collection was late at the post office, as mail used to take about a week to get to us from home. What all servicemen and women dreaded was the 'Dear John' letter, telling you that your romance was over. Fortunately, Joan never missed the post and I got my fair share of love letters from my darling girl.

CHAPTER 19

Concert Party

Sometime during the spring of 1951, word filtered down that there was talk of peace and the war came to a sudden halt for armistice negotiations that unfortunately failed. Brigadier Brodie (who commanded the 29th British Independent Infantry Brigade) sent for Major Andrews, our old concert-party producer, to round up the blokes from the ship coming out to Korea and form a concert party to entertain the troops. Willingly obeying orders, Andrews started to assemble a troop and told my captain, Recce Newcombe, that I was to go back to Seoul to join the concert party. At first, Newcombe held his ground and said something along the lines of not on your nelly, but Andrews countered with, 'It's the brigadier's orders.' After some banter, I was eventually let go. Later, Andrews confided in me that Newcombe had told him he had always fancied a certain hard-to-get fur hat, in limited supply at the time. As it turned out, Major Andrews had access to one of these delightful headpieces, so he asked Newcombe, 'Would you like one?' and Newcombe bit his hand off. 'Okay,' Andrews replied, 'if I give you one then I get Thackery.' The deal was done and I was swapped for a hat!

And so I packed up my gear and headed off to Seoul with Major Andrews and the concert party. We established ourselves in a theatre that had been damaged by bombs. It still had a stage and an area where we could sleep. The streets were deserted and there was an eerie calm. It was such a strange environment to be in, but we made this place our base and got reacquainted with each other. The boys were back!

Then Major Andrews told me he wanted to make me his second in command, 'I'm going to make you a bombardier, you'll be my assistant,' he said, adding, 'Go and find me a piano.'

'Where on earth am I going to find a piano?' I replied. Andrews dismissed my concern. 'Thack, I want a piano, just go and find me one now.'

And so we did. We jumped into a three-tonne truck and toured the deserted city in search of the instrument. Eventually we came across the city's university building. After a hunt through the corridors, we found what we were looking for and 'borrowed it'. Removing its legs, we carefully walked it down the stairs, determined not to damage it and committed to returning it in pristine condition once we had done with it.

My mate from Brancepeth, Sefton Smith, was among the gang, so we had an amazing pianist who could turn his hand to any song. Name a tune and he'd be able to play it. He was quite astonishing. He could also tune a piano, so he was vital to the success of the party. Rehearsals soon got underway on the stage and we were able to light the theatre using electricity pumped in from an American warship.

It was here that I met a chap called John Coleman Wood. He was a few years older than me and a wartime soldier in the Royal

Army Service Corps, who had done a bit of stage work. He had this marvellous ability to write parodies that made fun of what was going on. The pair of us formed a partnership and called ourselves 'A couple of swells', after a song we used to sing. I don't know where Major Andrews got all this gear from, but we had suits, battered straw hats and all sorts that we wore as we performed. We became quite famous, actually, and we even sang on the American Forces Network (the US forces' radio network). A lot of these songs took the mickey out of the Americans, but they took it all in good heart.

Piling onto two trucks, the concert party started to tour the troops and perform. We were very well received as the chaps hadn't had any entertainment for a long time, not even radios. We went all over the brigade area. It was hard work, as we did everything ourselves. but it was great fun.

A short time later, Major Andrews told us that we had been asked to escort and protect artists from ENSA (the Entertainments National Service Association, which provided entertainment from the Second World War on), while being their support act too. Soldiers liked to call it 'Every Night Something Awful'. All the big stars were signed up to ENSA, so we began to welcome artists such as Danny Kaye, whom we supported at some of the shows. It was so exciting to meet star names like that and we were all easily starstruck.

Another chap who came out and joined us was a famous British comedian called Jack Warner, who later played the title role in the hit TV show, *Dixon Of Dock Green*. He was great, an all-rounder who sang, did a bit of comedy and was an absolute hoot. Jack was greeted on his arrival by the mayor and mayoress of Seoul, whom he seemed very honoured to meet. Only, it wasn't the mayoral couple at all – it was actually two of our blokes dressed up as them, but they really did look the part. A bloke called Taffy Webb was dressed up as the mayoress in a Korean hat and gown and pretended to speak Korean while I played an interpreter, translating what was being said. Jack didn't have the foggiest what was going on. But when he went to shake the hand of the mayor, Barry, who was playing him, said in a broad cockney voice, 'Allo Jack, 'ow you goin' mate?' Jack nearly fell over, roaring with laughter, and thought the ruse was absolutely hilarious. He even wrote in his memoirs about 'those boys' and how he was taken in at this reception by the so-called mayor and mayoress of Seoul!

Jack Warner was a fluent French speaker, so we asked him if he would do a show for the Vingt Deux – the Royal Canadian 22nd Regiment (or, as they were called, the 'Van Doos'). When he got up on stage and started telling jokes in French, they were amazed. He really was such a good sport, just like one of us, even though he was a massive star at the time.

At another show, magician Robert Harbin stunned crowds with his magic tricks, including that old-time favourite trick of cutting someone in half. I assisted him night after night and, even though I was right there next to him, I still couldn't work out how he did it. And, as much as I begged him to, he wouldn't let me into any of his trade secrets.

All these shows took place in any open space that we could find where we could set up a stage. Sometimes we'd take over some kind of a building if we could fit the men in. Sometimes the staging would be made up of oil drums, though we did accumulate a lot of stuff to set up our own staging.

As well as entertaining the troops, our other role as a concert party was to protect the stars, just in case anything untoward ever took place. The peace negotiations then failed and the war restarted. So we were just keeping the peace in case it kicked off again. And didn't it just.

Major Andrews pulled me and some of the men aside and told me we were going back to our unit to support the Glosters. Apparently, it looked like they were going to come face to face with the enemy at a place called Imjin. I was devastated by the news as I really thought the war was over and because, dare I say it, I was enjoying being part of the concert party. But orders were orders and this is what we were there for, so me and a couple of other fellas jumped into a jeep and started to make our way back to meet our unit. The journey was long and in honesty we didn't really know what was going to happen. I was aware that we were going to go into battle – that's what we were trained to do – but we didn't know what the plan of attack was. As I've said, we troops were often the last to know. If we were going into an attack with the infantry we'd be brought into an 'O' group, which was an 'orders' group. Captain Newcombe would be told what was on the agenda and then he would gather us together and tell us what was what and what we might expect to see ahead of us.

As we neared our destination, the speeding jeep was brought to a sudden halt by some military policemen. To our consternation, they told us we couldn't go any further. We explained that we were supposed to meet our unit and I was to assume my observation post role. It was then that they told us the news that would haunt me to this day. They explained that the battle had been ferocious and the Glosters had fought heroically, but ultimately in vain, and the majority had been killed or taken prisoner. We couldn't believe what we were hearing. We had so many colleagues we knew there, not particularly closely, mind, but well enough to chat with and say hello to. The idea that many of the men we had been supporting during this operation had been killed or held captive broke our hearts.

The detail of what the Glosters did at Imjin would go down in British military history as one of the bloodiest and most heroic engagements outside the world wars. Around three-thousand men made up the United Nations forces – consisting of the Glosters, the Royal Ulster Rifles and the Royal Northumberland Fusiliers, as well as Belgian forces and other supporting units. They had been deployed along 12 miles of the Imjin River to block the popular invasion route to Seoul.

They had been expecting to face a major onslaught from the Chinese, but did not know quite how big, or how soon they'd arrive. The Chinese surprised them by arriving a day earlier than they'd expected, at around midnight on 22 April 1951, having marched 17 miles to the river's edge without stopping along the way. Their plan was to capture Seoul as a 'May Day gift' to Mao Zedong. Our troops were shocked to see that the Chinese had sent around ten-thousand men and so were a little unprepared, to say the least.

Intelligence had reported that the Chinese were filling in anti-tank ditches on approach roads and trying to fool the troops by setting off smoke clouds to hide their army's approach. The Glosters, however, were unaware that Chinese units had them under surveillance from Kamak-san, the 2,000-foot peak that separated the Glosters from the rest of the line of defence.

At midnight, the main body of the Chinese division crossed the river. In response, the Glosters fired at the approaching Chinese, but couldn't halt their progress. Over the next day or so, Chinese forces marched across the clifftops overlooking the river valley and fired at the Glosters from what had once been their own prepared hilltop positions, ultimately surrounding them and giving them no place to run.

A Chinese machine-gun post was set up on the key summit of Castle Hill. Lieutenant Philip Curtis, it has been said, bravely ran forward wielding a pistol in one hand and a grenade in the other in an attempt to take out the Chinese position. Miraculously, he made it through the first wave of fire, but was killed by the second. His grenade, however, fell into the Chinese area and managed to destroy it. He received a posthumous Victoria Cross for his heroism.

The next day, the Glosters were almost out of ammunition, yet the Chinese onslaught was relentless as they surrounded them. With so few arms left, the Brits tried to be clever. They had worked out that the Chinese used trumpets to direct their battalions in lieu of radios, so the Glosters were instructed to sound a range of British calls to confuse the enemy. And it worked – for a time.

The US commanders knew the only way of helping the Glosters was to break into the Chinese troop's tight circle. But doing so could endanger the whole line of defence.

It is said that the US Major General Robert H Soule asked our British brigadier, Thomas Brodie, 'How are the Glosters doing?' to which he replied, 'A bit sticky, things are pretty sticky down there.' Upon hearing that, the Americans, not used to good old-fashioned British understatement, took this to mean that the situation wasn't as bad as they had thought and so told the Glosters to stay put.

This was a disastrous move and, by this point, around a hundred of the six-hundred-and-fifty men were either dead or too injured to continue. All that was left was to try to make a run for it and reach the American positions a few miles to the rear. Only forty men escaped. The rest – radio operators and gunners – became prisoners of war.

Today, Hill 235 – upon which the regiment had fought so bravely – is called Gloster Hill. The Gloucester Regiment and 45th Field Regiment of the Royal Artillery were later awarded a US Presidential citation – the highest US award for heroism.

Still in shock from the devastating aftermath of that battle, we were sent back to another unit and, as we travelled in silence, it dawned on us that my observation post party had been involved in the battle and, had we got there an hour or so earlier, we too could have been imprisoned or even killed.

Years later, I was given a Peace medal by the Korean government for our time in the war. The Korean people still remember everything that happened and are still ever so grateful. I'm very proud of the medal but, as it was issued by another government, I cannot wear it on my uniform, which is a shame because it's a lovely medal.

Not long after this, our regiment was asked to withdraw from Korea and we were sent to Hong Kong, where I was finally able to start married life properly. The war raged on, ending eventually in July 1953. I, however, never returned to Korea.

PART 6

A soldier's life

CHAPTER 20

Reunited in Hong Kong

In 1952, a few months after I was posted to Hong Kong, Joan came out to join me. This was the first time she had ever been away from home, so she came with trepidation and excitement. Naturally enough, her mother Alice was beside herself with worry because none of her daughters had ever left Durham before and now here was one travelling across the world all by herself. Nobody flew in those days so poor Joan was stuck on a ship for a month. She was travelling by herself, but she managed to befriend two female army sergeants and another civilian lady who turned out to be the wife of one of our sergeants.

I was stationed in a base in the New Territories about 30 miles from Kowloon and our main role as soldiers was to keep the peace and protect the British colony. Before Joan had started on her journey I had applied for married quarters, but to qualify I needed to fulfil certain criteria of rank, age and time married. As we fulfilled none of these, I had to find a place for the two of us to live instead and pay for it out of my own pocket. After a hasty search in the local newspapers, I came across a cosy little one-bedroom flat down in Kowloon, a few miles away from camp. It wasn't ideal but it was cheap and it would mean that I would have to go up to the camp in a truck every day. The rental price also included a 'cook boy', who would prepare meals for us out in the yard. I wasn't sure if Joan would be happy about having someone cook for us as she was such an independent woman, but I thought it might be nice to let someone look after her following her long journey. As it would turn out, he was a very good cook.

When the ship pulled into the docks at Kowloon, I could see Joan on the deck, stretching over the railing trying to find me. Then she spotted me and started waving like a mad woman, a huge smile on her face and tears of joy rolling down her cheeks. She looked more beautiful than I remembered and I couldn't wait to scoop her up into my arms and give her a long-awaited kiss. It felt like an age waiting for the ship to dock and the passengers to disembark, but eventually I saw her dashing through the crowd. Before I even got to plant a big smacker on her lips, she said to me in her dry Durham accent, 'Hey, Hunk, you have a bald patch.' I was horrified. Had I? But, before I could respond, she added, 'If I never hear bagpipes again, it'll be too soon.' It turned out that the Scottish regiment The Black Watch had been on board, heading out to Korea, and had been making one 'hell of a noise' all day and all night.

As I took her back to the flat, I simply couldn't tear my eyes away from her. She had not changed at all. She was still my Joan and she was still the prettiest lady I had ever seen. The girl I had married two years before.

We had only been together for such a short time before I had departed for Korea, so I suppose we were a bit nervous about re-establishing our relations. But we soon overcame any doubts we shared and started to go out to enjoy our favourite pastime, which was, of course, dancing.

So, despite being apart for such a long time, we soon felt comfortable with each other and settled into a routine. I had to head up to the camp early in the morning. In the Far East, we'd always have an early start, around 6am and be on duty until about 1pm. That meant I'd have to get up at an ungodly hour to get a truck up to the camp, but I didn't mind – having Joan by my side made up for any inconveniences. My responsibilities at the camp during these shifts were vehicle maintenance as well as training. Sometimes we would go out on patrol in the mountains and climb up the observation posts to look out into communist 'red' China.

After a few weeks of pottering around our tiny flat, Joan was itching to get a job. I could understand that. The place was pretty cramped and I was away most of the day, so she must have felt very cooped up. The house that the flat was in belonged to a delightful Chinese woman whom we suspected of having an affair with a very charming French gent we kept seeing around the place. Joan got chatting to him one day and mentioned in passing that she was on the lookout for a job and that her experiences had been mainly in retail. As a favour, he said he'd drop a note to the managing director of the department store Lane Crawford (they were friends apparently). Lane Crawford was a wonderful high-end store, a bit like Harrods for Hong Kong at the time. Within a week Joan had received word that she had landed a job in one of the store's luxury jewellery departments, which was mainly frequented by visitors off the cruise ships. It was a great job and the wage was even better – Joan was earning three times more than me! She used to travel from Kowloon to Hong Kong Island every day on the ferry – to save money she used to travel with the hundreds of Chinese workers on the lower decks, when most Westerners travelled on the upper decks. Being small and dark-haired, she was virtually indistinguishable from the locals.

When we weren't working, Joan and I loved socializing. We would eat out all the time and usually spent more than we actually earned. One of our favourite places was the Dairy Farm restaurant on Kowloon High Street. In the hot weather we'd drink Honolulu Coolers. They were lovely. I used to love their T-bone steaks too – they were enormous!

Joan enjoyed going to the pictures to see big romantic films and, whenever we could, we'd go dancing. Oh, how we still loved to dance – and sing, of course. Singing was very important in our world. At home we'd be singing all the time.

We made so many friends in Kowloon, but we got really close to one of the soldiers from my regiment whom I'd known for a while.

Ken Brown was a delightful guy whom I'd first met at Brancepeth a couple of years ago. At the time, the sergeant major had issued me with the mission 'to smarten him up' – just like he had with Sefton Smith. He thought the young fella was a bit too 'funny' for the Army. In fairness, he could certainly talk for England and I think his wacky character wasn't quite what the officers were after. But he was such a charmer and I knew one day that that charm would pay dividends for him. Dutifully, I showed Ken the ropes and made sure he was a good fit for the regiment and, as a result, a good friendship blossomed between us, mainly because we both shared the same daft sense of humour.

Before Joan joined us in Kowloon, Ken and I would hang out in the town a lot. We'd go to the bars and attend the talent show that was held regularly at the China Fleet Club in Kowloon. On one occasion, when Ken wasn't able to join me as he was working, I went on my own. I loved this place as it was a great chance to see some really talented folk. I had tried my luck a few times and did fairly well. But on this particular night, a fella got up on stage whose voice just blew me away.

His name was Lance Corporal Terry Parsons and he was a member of the Royal Army Service Corps. He drove trucks in the Army but, back home in London, he drove a bus. When I saw Ken next. I said to him, 'Ken, you have to see this guy. He is a phenomenal singer. I think he could be going places. He's the British Frank Sinatra! Mark my words.' The next time we were both free, we headed back to the China Fleet Club and, as luck would have it, Parsons was back on stage creating magic. Ken agreed that the fella had something special about him. He also turned out to be a nice chap and really serious about singing, so it came as no surprise when we learned a little time after that he had quit the Army and headed back to Blighty to pursue a singing career. And it worked out for him too. He became a massive superstar who went on to record one of the best James Bond themes ever. What do you mean you haven't heard of him? Oh yes, when he got back to the UK, Terry Parsons changed his name to Matt Monro and the rest, as they say, is history. In 1956 Matt got his first record deal with Decca. And a mere 63 years later

I would do the same! As a postscript to the story, Ken and Matt tried to form a double act a few years later but, sadly for Ken, it never worked out. He did, however, make a surprise appearance on TV for Matt Monro when he was on *This Is Your Life* in 1977.

Anyway, where was I? Oh yes, so Ken became a very good friend and loved Joan when she came over to join us. She thought he was a real card too. We forged a really close bond and had a lot of fun together. Ken, who was single, told me that he loved the relationship Joan and I had and that he wanted one just like ours, so while we were camped there in Hong Kong, Ken started to court a lovely girl called Joan (yes, another one!). She was the daughter of the local government official, who had made it quite clear to Ken that he wasn't keen on soldier boys in the slightest. In fact, he thought that soldiers had crawled out from under a stone and wholly objected to their union. For a while, they had to run around secretly and hang around with Joan and me. We were quite the double daters. But then, the government official retired from his post and took Joan and his family to Australia. I think Ken and his Joan stayed in touch for the next five years and, when he left the Army, he headed to Australia, tracked her down and married her. Based permanently down under, he landed a job in sales at a confectionery company called Nestlé, where his sparkling wit helped him rise quickly through the ranks in this famous firm.

CHAPTER 21

Jolted into adulthood

In 1953, after about a year or so of falling over each other in our tiny flat, Joan and I thought it was time to find a bigger place. Now that Joan was earning a fair whack, we could actually afford somewhere a little roomier. Flicking through the *China Morning Post*, which is where all the best properties were advertised, we found a slightly larger flat that came complete with a housemaid called Margaret.

And just in the nick of time, too, because Joan then discovered she was pregnant. I couldn't believe what I was hearing as we certainly hadn't planned it, but it made me the happiest man alive. Joan's joy, however, was bittersweet, as her mother Alice was all the way across the world and she really wanted her to be there.

Aside from a sense of unadulterated joy, the news had another effect on me – it suddenly jolted me into adulthood. I was still a bit of a twit, if I'm honest, but then I was still shy of 25. Knowing that in a few months' time I was going to be a dad and responsible for a human being, albeit a little one, was just the wake-up call I needed.

Frustratingly, just as it looked as though I was on an upward trajectory, I had a setback that knocked me back. I'd only recently gained my first stripe, which gave me the title lance bombardier. I was thrilled, of course, because it meant I was making small steps within the regiment. However, just before Joan announced her pregnancy, I suddenly lost my cherished stripe. I had been 'loaned' to the battery commanding officer as a driver operator. One of my duties was to ferry the lieutenant colonel around. He asked me to take him to one of the gun positions in a lovely scout car called a Dingo, a tiny car that moved like the wind. When we got to the gun position, we found that a chap had got his hand caught in the breach of a gun and it didn't look pretty. Concerned that the fella might lose his hand, the lieutenant colonel said, 'Get him off the gun, pop him in the Dingo and get him to the hospital as fast as you can.' So I did.

As I was heading back, I heard the lieutenant colonel's voice again on the radio, giving the regiment orders to move, so I put my foot down in order to get back to the gun position as fast as possible. What I didn't think about at the time was that there was a very strict speed limit of thirty miles per hour throughout the New Territories and I was doing sixty! I probably would have got away with it if it wasn't for the fact that the brigadier's car happened to be on the same road, not far behind me, and his driver had taken down the number of the Dingo and reported it. I couldn't believe my rotten luck. I was trying to do the right thing and I got punished for it instead. What are the chances? I was charged with speeding and had to go up before the battery commander, who had the rank of major. I was told that he wasn't able to deal with the case because it was a brigadier's charge. So I was then sent up before the very colonel whom I had been driving around in the first place. When he saw me, he thought it was a right old hoot. 'A couple of weeks ago, I was giving you a commendation. Now I have to take a stripe off you!' I was gutted by the decision, but rules are rules. I actually think I got the stripe back about six weeks later. This is so typical of the Army – following the rules by docking me my stripe, but giving it back shortly after due to mitigating circumstances!

Being heavily pregnant didn't slow Joan down in the slightest. We got in with a civilian crowd and used to go dancing all the time. In fact, we spent all our money on it. When we were short of cash, which was generally at the end of the month, we used to go to a very cheap Russian restaurant called Katchenkos where we'd feast on borscht – Russian peasant soup made from beetroot. It was delicious and very nutritious, I could eat it now. And pregnancy didn't stop my Joan from working. Far from it – she carried on at Lane Crawford, waddling around until she was almost ready to give birth.

There was a wonderful and much-needed sense of jubilation when news reached camp that our boys, who'd been taken prisoner at the Battle of Imjin River, had finally been released. Everyone was over the moon. We were told that the prisoners were being brought to Kowloon and the remaining veterans of the Korea campaign would host them for the afternoon while they were on shore leave. I was one of the group asked to look after our newly released POWs. Before we set off to the docks to be assigned some soldiers, we were closely briefed about what they were allowed to have. We were told they had to avoid certain foods in case it upset their stomachs and I was asked if I could take Joan along because the fellas were desperate to talk to an English woman. When we arrived at the docks to pick up our charges, the atmosphere was electric. Everyone was so pleased that our brave men were coming home after their incarceration.

The former prisoners arrived on a troopship instead of a battleship so they could get accustomed to normal life again. It took the poor fellas a week to get to us, so they were very eager to get off the ship and see some friendly faces. As Joan and I watched the ship drift into dock, I wondered what life in a prison must have been like for the boys and thought how lucky we were not to have been caught up in that terrible battle.

As the troops came ashore, we were assigned four of them, who rushed past me to greet Joan. They didn't care about anything I had to say, but they treated her like royalty because she was so pregnant at the time. The men had a three-hour window before we had to deliver them to the NAFFI (the Navy, Army and Air Force Institute that runs the shops and cafés across the British armed forces) club for their welcome-home meal. They asked if Joan would help them buy gifts for their wives and girlfriends, but when she tried to get them to be more specific, they went coy until one of them said, 'Underwear!' Quietly amused, Joan dutifully helped them out, guiding them around the lingerie department in a local store. 'So, lads,' she said. 'What size busts have your girls got?' Of course, like most fellas, they had absolutely no idea and muttered, 'About your size.' Joan laughed, 'But I'm pregnant!' We had such a lot of laughs that day. She sorted lots of things for them, then we took them back to the NAFFI club and had a meal together. Before we knew it, it was time to get on the bus and get them back to the ship so they could go home armed with their bags of underwear!

CHAPTER 22

Dawn of a new era

One day our housemaid Margaret said to me, 'Master, you give me silver coin.' And I said, 'Yes, of course, here you go,' and handed her a bright, shiny coin. The next day, she asked the same thing. Again, I was only too happy to oblige. But when she asked me for a third time, a fourth and a fifth, I was curious. Were we not paying her enough? Was she in trouble?

Sensitively, I asked her, 'Margaret, is everything alright?'

'Yes, Mr Colin,' she replied.

'Why then have you been asking for silver coins for the past week?'

Margaret giggled. 'Mr Colin, I go to the temple. I pray that your baby have fifty strong sons.'

I wasn't quite sure how to react but thanked her for her kind thoughts and prayed myself that if we had a baby girl, she wouldn't have that many children. Years later, when Dawn married her husband, I gave him a scare when I told him about Margaret's prayers. To say he was alarmed is an understatement.

After we'd seen the released POWs off back home, life got back to normal again. Joan continued to get larger by the day. Even though it was hard going for her, she still chose to go to work at the department store. Every so often she would have regular medical checks at the British Military Hospital in Kowloon. It was fully staffed with nurses, sisters and midwives, so Joan felt comfortable about her upcoming birth, bearing in mind she wouldn't have her own mother there holding her hand during the procedure. However, during her tests, the doctor told her that she may have something called cephalopelvic disproportion. Because her pelvis was smaller than usual there was a possibility that it might be more difficult to have a natural birth and could mean she'd have to have a Caesarean. Joan was unfazed by the news and said she'd face it when she had to. However, when they asked her if she wanted to know the sex of the baby, she shut them down straightaway and said she'd rather find out when the baby was born. I agreed. I never understand why people insist on finding out if they are having a boy or girl. It should be a lovely surprise.

With just a couple of weeks to the birth, we carried on life as best we could, having meals out, going to the pictures and all sorts. We had been given a date and it was still a little way off.

For the past few weeks, I had been going to judo classes that took place on the roof of the building that we lived in. The classes were run by a little Japanese instructor who was very serious and amusingly strict. As I was quite proficient at judo, the instructor asked if I would take part in a judo demonstration for the Hong Kong police at their sports club and I was happy to oblige. I was matched against a rather large naval officer. I can't remember the name of the move I was demonstrating – I think it was a hip throw. Because our statures were very different, I wasn't sure if I could manage the move I was being asked to do, but I gave it a go and miraculously I managed to throw him over. However, as he hit the ground, we could hear his arm pop out of the socket, followed by painful screaming. While everyone was in a panic about the poor chap's arm, the instructor calmly ordered everyone to sit on top of him. After a moment's hesitation, we all piled on, the instructor made a couple of swift manoeuvres and, within seconds, my opponent's shoulder was back in place. Afterwards, the chap apologized and told us that he had a weak shoulder!

When I arrived home, Joan was sitting in the living room with a friend. After welcoming me home, she casually added, 'I think it's time we went to the hospital, I think the baby is coming.' It turned out she was in the middle of having contractions. I raced her to the car and drove her to the British Military Hospital where we were taken straight to the maternity ward, which was run by a rather formidable female major.

She began asking Joan a series of questions to see how far into labour she was. Then she glanced at me, as if seeing me for the first time, and offered me a withering, 'Yes?'

'Where can I go and sit?' I muttered.

'What do you mean, sit?' she said matter-of-factly. 'Do you think you're going to stay with her?'

'Yes, mam,' I replied, earnestly.

'Oh no you're not!' she snapped. 'Now go away. It's an order. Call me in the morning.'

Reluctantly, I said my goodbyes to Joan, whispered, 'See you in the morning,' into her belly and watched the major lead her away. I went back home, gritting my teeth.

So, on the morning of 27 September 1953, around 6am, the hospital called to tell me that our baby daughter had been born around midnight. Well, or so they thought. The nurses couldn't actually work out if she had been delivered before or after midnight. I couldn't quite understand why they had a problem deciding, but I chose to ignore that and took time to be a proud father. I was so excited that I got my stuff together, drove to the hospital and waited my turn to go in and see mother and daughter. Dawn was just beautiful, lying with her mother. She was a small baby, which was fortunate for Joan with her small pelvis. Joan was doing well and said the birth had been relatively easy. Of course, births were second nature to her. She had grown up with her younger sisters being born at home, and her two eldest sisters having their own babies at home too.

When Joan came back to the flat, I could tell that she really missed having her mam around during those first few days of motherhood. Luckily, Joan had some close friends nearby who would help her during her most stressful moments.

Even though Dawn was just a tiny thing, it took us a few days to adjust to having a new member of the family in our small home. Dawn was a good baby who rarely cried, but her sleeping patterns were very different to ours!

While Joan and I were jubilant about baby Dawn, Margaret was beside herself with joy. She loved our little girl as if she were her own. When she'd take her out and about in her pram, she would tell passers-by, 'This is my English baby.' When she'd meet other housemaids pushing their own 'English' babies around, they'd all claim that their baby was prettier than all the others. Sometimes there would a jovial battle between Joan and Margaret over who'd look after Dawn, and sometimes Joan would have to say, 'But that's my job.' But, all in all, Margaret was a godsend. She was great for babysitting and was always was so reliable. When Dawn was no longer breastfeeding and had moved on to bottles, we'd go out more and let Margaret look after her. She absolutely adored Dawn.

A little while after Dawn's birth, I was told that our regiment was being relieved by another regiment and being sent back to the UK. It was exciting news because it had been such a long time since any of us had been home. Joan was particularly excited because it meant that her mam and family would finally get to meet their new family member.

CHAPTER 23

Married life and fun in the mess

After a month-long journey Joan and I were pleased to be back on UK soil. The ship docked in Liverpool and when we came ashore we were met by an army of mums and dads all eagerly trying to find their sons and daughters. Joan's parents had travelled all the way from County Durham carrying a Moses basket full of clothes and hot-water bottles. I don't know what Mam thought we were doing to our child – she must have thought we were going to bring the baby back naked. As soon as she saw Dawn, she was beside herself with joy. She grabbed her from Joan and cradled her, reeling off all the dos and don'ts that new mums should be wary of. Dawn was about four or five months old by now and Joan seemed to have the mum thing down pat, but she let Mam off because she knew how excited she was to see her new grandchild.

Joan and Dawn went back to Durham with the family, while I joined the rest of my regiment on a train down to Kirkee and McMunn Barracks in Colchester, where I was promoted to bombardier, which is the traditional Royal Artillery name for the rank of corporal.

When I arrived at our new barracks, I was excited to have been allotted our very first married quarters. It was a ground-floor flat, but the place was far from cosy and romantic. On the contrary, in the bedroom there was a rifle block and a steel cabinet where soldiers would hang their kit. It looked more like a barracks room than a family home. When Joan joined me, she saw the funny side about the rifle block but, nevertheless, we swiftly got it taken away.

Although we had only been apart a few days, I had really missed Joan and Dawn. Before they arrived, I spent a good few hours giving the quarters a thorough scrub, so it was spick and span. I knew Joan would expect nothing less. When she walked through the door, however, the first thing she said was, 'This place needs a bit of a tidy-up.' I was gutted, 'I've been slaving away!'

The living conditions were adequate but certainly nothing special. There was no central heating back then, and the water for the bath and laundry ran from a big, fat boiler. There was no garden, as such, so to dry her washing Joan would climb out of the window and hang it on a line in this gap between buildings.

Luckily, we only stayed in Colchester for about five months before the regiment was sent out to Dortmund in Germany. There was no particular reason why we went there, regiments get sent to places all the time. In stark contrast to the quarters in Colchester, the German barracks was large and our marital flat, which was on the first floor, was very modern. We were entitled to an A-type quarter, which was a one-bedroom flat. Because I was a bombardier, I was considered a senior figure within the block of flats we lived in, regardless of who else lived there – not all residents were from my regiment. Not everyone in the building, however, respected my authority. One particular night, Joan and I were stirred by an almighty row taking place in one of the flats above us. It actually sounded like the fella was beating up his other half, so I stormed upstairs and started rapping on the door, trying to bring about some peace. When the door opened, however, it was the wife who gave me an earful, telling me to keep my nose out.

We weren't in the flat for long, though, as it was here that I got my third stripe and then had use of the Sergeants' Mess, where the unmarried sergeants were quartered, and we could eat and socialize with colleagues of the same rank. It was a place of entertainment for us and our wives. In Germany I was a gun sergeant, so responsible for a 25-pound gun and all the equipment that came with it. I had six men in my section – almost everyone was on national service – including three miners from Wales. Boy, could they dig gun pits.

One afternoon Joan and I were sitting in our quarters when one of my chaps knocked on the door. 'Excuse me, Sarge,' he said urgently. 'Your daughter's sitting on the windowsill.' I rushed out, telling my mates to stay downstairs in case she fell. We had to tread carefully because we were scared to frighten her – she would have been less than two years old at the time. I slipped my shoes off and crept into the bedroom where the window was open because it was summertime. She was dangling her legs out, happy as Larry! I was horrified. It was a first-floor flat, so high enough that the fall could have killed her, but she was smiling away at everyone. She didn't understand why this bloke was standing under the window. I was so grateful to those two fellas that day for preventing an awful accident. I managed to get her in safely and I dread to think what would have happened if they hadn't been there.

My job as a sergeant kept me very busy. Apart from our battery and regimental duties, there'd be times when we'd be on the rota to be guard commander, which was a 24-hour job.

Looking after the people in your charge was important too. These lads relied on each other. I found myself running a floor in the barracks where there were about thirty or forty men. My responsibility was to go in first thing in the morning. The bombardier below me would wake them up so they were ready to go when I arrived, then I would get them out on parade and check them. I also had to make sure that all the tasks that had been detailed to people – such as cleaning the toilet and so on – had been done.

But sometimes it wasn't always checked. Not long after we'd moved in, all the soldiers had gone out on parade and the medical officer (MO) was making his rounds. His first job was to inspect the conditions, but he was only interested in the loos. My battery sergeant major was an amusing chap – we became quite good friends. This particular morning, the loos were in a right old state. One had a crack in it and the second had the biggest piece of excrement I'd ever seen in my life. Boy, this chap had done a crap so large that he couldn't flush it, so he dashed off and left it.

The doctor was looking in the loos and Dennis, the sergeant major, thought he was looking at the one with the crack in it. The doctor said, 'Good gracious! How long has this been here?' Dennis stammered nervously, 'Sorry, sir, it was like that when we took over a couple of months ago and we have reported it.' But the doctor had been looking at the crap, not the crack!

Luckily, the doctor saw the funny side and we all started laughing. We never did find out who the culprit was!

Joan and I settled into life in the barracks, which were really nice, with great, long corridors and lovely married quarters. And we weren't too far from the attractions of the city of Dusseldorf. So soon after the Second World War, relations between the Germans and the troops were understandably a little strained – not so much with the older folk, but more with the younger element. Very occasionally, fights would break out between the Germans and our lads in the bars, but in most cases it wasn't anything too serious. As far as we were concerned, there was no anger any more. By now, almost ten years had gone by and we were just there to do our jobs and keep the peace. Our memories of the war were behind us and we didn't hold grudges. Obviously some people did harbour hatred, but the way we saw it, the war was in the past.

We had a very strict regimental sergeant major (RSM) in the 45th Regiment – Douglas Ward. He was a very famous RSM in his day – D J Ward MBE – and he was a great guy, but very strict. His rules for running the mess were simple and you didn't break them. You could say what you liked in the mess – swear, tell dirty jokes – but the moment a woman walked in, you zipped it. You don't swear in front of women. And you had to be dressed right at all times. Mess rules stated that you had to wear uniform and if you were wearing a hat you would take it off. If you had a cane, you would put it to one side before you came into the bar. If you were in civilian clothes, you had to wear a jacket and your regimental tie. These days, it's a lot more relaxed, but in my day everything had to be done properly.

I still can't go into a mess without wearing a collar, tie and a jacket. Habits are hard to break.

Every month, there was a formal mess dinner with all the silver cutlery and it was quite an occasion. You'd attend in blues, the old-fashioned uniforms, buttoned up to the neck and sit down to a proper dinner. I remember it clearly to this day. The tables were in a U shape and Douglas would always sit at the top table because he was the most senior mess member. Everyone would be seated according to their rank, so the more junior you were, the further along you were. When I was a young junior sergeant, I would sit far away but directly in Douglas's line of sight at the end of one of the legs so I had to mind my manners! There was a tradition of toasting the Queen so it was a good idea to have a pee before you went in because you couldn't go anywhere until the loyal toast was over. That came after the main course, so no matter how desperate you were to go, you'd have to damn well sit there. At some point in the evening, someone would give Douglas the signal and he'd take up his gavel and bang it on the table, saying, 'Sergeant Vice, Her Majesty The Queen.' This was a signal for the loyal toast to be given by the youngest sergeant, who is always termed sergeant vice.

I'll never forget the night that Joan came to her first formal mess. She was so excited because she got the chance to dress up and put her make-up on, and she looked beautiful. But she was also a little bit nervous because she knew there were certain rules and etiquette at the table. I was so proud to have Joan there with me and she took her place at the table next to me. On her left was a friend of mine, who was a lovely chap. Now Joan was left-handed and never did

The Thackery family in 1960, with baby Peter and Dawn at
the Sergeants' Mess Children's Christmas Party in Germany.

A family trip to the mountains in
Hong Kong in a trusty Ford Consul.

This is me as a young Sergeant in #13 Dress – a combination of the
#1 trousers and #3 white top. I was the Sergeant in charge of
the Honour Guard at the British Embassy.

Instructing a Gunner regiment on the ranges in Yorkshire with the Territorial
Army c.1955. I was the only regular soldier in Barnsley at the time.

THE NORFOLK OPERA PLAYERS

Me as Dr Caius and Joan as part of the
Chorus in *The Merry Wives of Windsor.*

Joan and me in one of our first
productions as villagers in
Verdi's *Nabucco.*

Me as the General and Joan as the Matron
in Gilbert and Sullivan's *Trial by Jury.*

Joan and me singing 'I Remember it Well' at
our 50th wedding anniversary in 2000.

Singing 'Wind Beneath my Wings' to Joan at my 80th birthday in 2010.

Joan and her siblings at a gathering at the Masonic Ladies' Night near Liverpool. From left to right, top: Veronica, Winifred, Monica, Marie, Adele and Yvonne; front: Henry and Joan.

In the Sergeants' Mess at Larkhill, there's a board with all the 900+ names of those who were in the Boys' Service, Royal Artillery. No. 710 is Thackery, C. A.

Sharing Remembrance Day with future generations.
Me and my grandchildren Ollie and Honey. Ollie always liked to
wear my medals at the end of the parade when he was young.

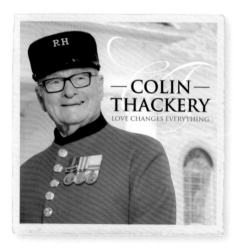

How could I ever have imagined that, at the age of 89, I would release
my first album with Decca and, on the occasion of my 90th birthday in
March 2020, will be on a nationwide tour?

Joan and me at Peter's wedding. Joan was buried in this beautiful red dress.

This is the picture that hangs on my berth wall, which I talk to every night.

My beautiful wife, Joan.

anything with her right. She even had left-handed scissors. As the evening went on, Joan relaxed and I could see she was enjoying herself, having a lovely chat with the chap next to her while she sipped from her glass. What she didn't realise was that she was actually drinking his wine. This went on for ages, until I felt a tap on my back. He was killing himself with laughter and whispered, 'She's drinking my bloody wine.' After that, Joan always made sure she used the wine glass on the right-hand side.

That night at the appropriate moment, the sergeant did the Queen's toast and carried out his duty as usual. A few weeks later, it was St David's Day so time for another celebration. Within the garrison were the Royal Welsh Fusiliers and we were invited to their mess, which was lovely. At the appropriate time, their sergeant vice toasted the Queen. And Joan turned to me and said, 'They have a Sergeant Vice as well. Isn't that a coincidence?'

We had a happy life at the station and Joan made a lot of friends there. She became pals with other sergeants' wives and sometimes they'd go out together. One of her best friends was Liz, who was married to Tony Prince, whom I got to know years before when we joined Boys' Service at the same time. Joan was also pals with another sergeant's wife called Jean and when we were on a long exercise in Germany, the girls would go back to England for a while. It's not always easy being an army wife, but Joan was very understanding. Sometimes these exercises would go on for ages, so it was good that she had so many friends. In fact, we both made friends for life while we were out there. My mate Tony wasn't in the same battery as me at the start so, although we had joined at the same time, we didn't

know each other well in the early army days. But our friendship grew the more time we spent with each other. When you're in the service, you need friends like him – someone who you can talk about all sorts with and confide in. I could tell Tony everything. Army life was hard work but also good fun – there was always something going on and I made such good friends during that time.

When I was sergeant major, I took my turn as president of the mess committee (PMC) and as a sergeant I'd take my turn as mess caterer. This meant I'd come off my regular duties to run the mess for a month, including the bar, which was good training for handling cash and accounts, but it meant I wouldn't get a chance to see my family because I'd be up early in the morning, stay to supervise things in the daytime and not get home until the bar closed. Those were long, busy days, but it was definitely worth it.

One of my favourite things to do was to organize a curry lunch on the Sunday, with a big family event at the station. While the adults sat down to eat their curry lunch, the children would watch films that came courtesy of the Army Kinema Corporation. We always made sure we had a good supply of movies the kids would like, such as Mickey Mouse or 'King of the cowboys', Roy Rogers. That kept the little ones occupied while their parents were eating.

Weekends were time for fun. Once a month, we'd have various dances on Saturdays, such as the tramp ball, pyjama parties or vicars and tarts – and you'd come dressed accordingly. The funniest one was 'Come as you find'. I'd send out one of my team to go around the married quarters at odd times during the day and night, and whenever the couple opened the door, he would make a note of how

they were dressed. Then they'd have to come to the party in that attire, which caused plenty of embarrassing moments! Some of the women were good sports and they'd come to the party with curlers in their hair. Of course, being a sergeant major was serious stuff when you were out on duty, but there were plenty of lighter moments to keep you going and it was such fun organizing those parties. Even our RSM Douglas Ward would come and join in.

There were lots of manoeuvres done in Germany. I think the reason why we were doing them was because we knew the Russians were also doing manoeuvres at the borders, so we wanted them to think we were still in control and ready for action. We'd behave as if we were at war, except we didn't fire live rounds, just blanks. One of the other battalions would play the enemy. It was just to keep us sharp.

CHAPTER 24

Bulls in Barnsley

From Germany I was posted to a territorial unit of part-time soldiers back home. For a fairly young sergeant, part of your development often involves training younger or part-time soldiers. So I was posted to 271st Regiment in Yorkshire as a personal staff instructor (PSI).

The regiment was based in Sheffield, but I was given a battery that consisted of six artillery guns and about a hundred men, on my own in Barnsley. Prior to this, I went on a marvellous course for three months at the Royal School of Artillery, which enabled me to teach all aspects of modern gunnery. When we arrived, the men immediately took a shine to Joan because she was from up that way, but I was a blooming southerner, so for about six weeks or so they held me at arm's length, but they did eventually accept me. Every TA unit has a local headquarters called a drill hall. In Barnsley, our married quarters consisted of a flat within the drill hall itself.

I had three civilian staff – the caretaker, who was ex-service, an ex-policeman, who looked after the vehicles, and another chap called limber gunner, whose job it was to look after the guns. Every week, I'd drive over to Sheffield to catch up on any business with the headquarters, including picking up the civilians' pay.

The major who commanded the battery was the director of a steel rolling mill. He was a very nice man. Most of the officers were civilians and being a soldier was like a hobby to them, which they did part-time.

It was a good job, but hard work. Everything had to be ready for drills in the evening or on a Sunday. I remember one afternoon when I'd just taken off my tunic and a police car pulled up outside. Joan went to the door and I heard a Yorkshire voice say, 'Is the sergeant in? Can I have a word?'

When I heard that, I was worried, so I went out to greet him.

He was a burly chap and he said, 'Have you got rifles and ammunition?'

I said, 'Yes, of course I have.'

'Can you get it?' he asked.

'No,' I replied. 'I don't have an officer here to authorize it.'

He replied that his inspector said he would cover for it.

'What's the problem?' I asked.

To my surprise, he replied, 'We have a mad bull we need you to kill.'

I went to one safe to get five bullets, then another to get the rifle – it took me a few minutes and then I put my tunic back on again.

'You might need to bring your Land Rover,' the man said. 'Because you may need to go off-road.'

I was given a police escort through the streets and I was met with a sight I hadn't come across before in my military life. This bull – and he was a huge beast – was near the end of his life, so was being taken to the slaughterhouse in the morning, but when he got the smell of it he had gone berserk and started frightening people. They'd been chasing him all day, trying to get him under control. By now it was tea time and the police were getting worried because he was in an open field and they could hear children playing nearby.

We got to this spot and they said, 'Is there anything we need to do?'

And I said, 'Yes, there are people all over – you need to get them out of the area.'

'Why?' he said.

'We have to be careful about the ricochet,' I said. 'We don't know exactly where the bullet's going to go.'

'Oh yes, I see what you mean,' he said, and went off to organize it.

'Where do I aim for?' I asked the butcher.

'We normally put the gun on the forehead,' he replied, so I aimed for that spot. But of course, the forehead is not only sloping, it's like an armoured car made of thick bone. I'm a good shot and I hit the bull straight on the forehead, but the bullet bounced right off. The result was that the bull got angrier and he started charging at me. At that point, I could see people starting to panic and I didn't blame them! Luckily, I was able to reload quickly and took another shot – this time I managed to hit him in the eye. He rolled over and over and I'd killed him. All of a sudden, I heard a cheer from behind. It turns out that while I'd been firing away, the crowd had gathered again and watched my every move. God knows where the ricochet went. This was no pop gun; this was a powerful 303 rifle.

Everything has to be accounted for, so I cleaned the rifle and put it away. I'd only used two or three of the bullets, so I put the remainder in the safe. I called headquarters next morning and explained to the training major what had happened. I think he was a bit shocked, as I shouldn't really have acted without Army authority, but the training major accepted that, under the circumstances and with the danger to the public, I had done the right thing in killing the bull.

Another time, the police came by again. I heard the familiar, 'Is the sergeant there?' and I thought, 'Oh God, what now? I hope it's not another bull.'

The man asked me to come and look at something in the boot of his car. I opened it and there in the boot was an anti-aircraft shell. It was a 40-millimetre shell from the Second World War. 'Can you take it?' he asked.

I was horrified. 'No, I'm not touching it!' I said. 'It's still live. There's explosive in the brass cartridge case of the shell and in the warhead itself.'

'So, what do you want us to do?' he asked. Clearly he had no idea how dangerous it was and I didn't want to panic him, but I knew he had to get away from it fast.

'I want you to drive slowly up to the yard, leave it in the middle and put a guard around it,' I said, as calmly as I could. 'Because if it goes off, it will wreck your car, but it's better than wrecking people. Meanwhile, I will send in the bomb disposal unit.'

It was a nerve-wracking time waiting for them, especially as it took them a while to arrive. When they came, the senior disposal expert was a sergeant.

'What's the trouble?' he asked. I explained it was a 40-millimetre shell and that it was probably going to be okay, but I had advised the policeman not to touch it. He immediately told the police he would have to blow it up right there. Very carefully, he took the shell out of the car and found a forty-gallon barrel, into which he put some sawdust. We backed away a little while he worked – I knew full well it could go off at any minute.

The bomb disposal unit set a charge to it and, with an enormous bang, it blew up. No one was more surprised than the police – they weren't to know what it was capable of. It turned out that someone had dug the thing up in his garden and phoned the police and asked them to take it away.

After this incident the police asked me to instruct the whole force on the working of ordnance so they would know not to move live munitions and to ask the Army's bomb disposal unit to come to the site of any find. That day, they had a lucky escape.

CHAPTER 25

And then we were four

In the autumn of 1959, we'd just had the happy news that Joan was pregnant again when I found out I was being posted to 14th Field Regiment at Barnard Castle in County Durham. Joan and I were over the moon to be having another baby, so we were hoping to get settled in our new home before the big day.

I was posted there as a survey sergeant for the regiment. I was given a survey party to look after and I was responsible for training the men who were doing national service. Two of them were teachers and two were accountants who had deferred their national service while training for their professions, so they had come back to do their time.

Before we moved, I was told there'd be no quarters because we would only be there for a short period, after which we were going to Hong Kong. So we had to find our own accommodation and pay rent. Joan's family found a house in a village called Howden-le-Wear in County Durham, which is about a mile south of the large market town of Crook. It had everything we needed: a few shops, including a convenience store, a hairdresser's, a butcher and the petrol station. We had a tiny little house that belonged to an old lady who was in hospital. It may have been small, but it was a sweet little place. I remember it had a huge aspidistra, one of those plants with the big leaves. Everyone had one back then.

We hadn't exactly planned the baby. I was quite content having Dawn, but my mother-in-law said she wouldn't be happy with us just having one child and neither should we. She was determined that Dawn should have a brother or sister, and she was right. I'm so glad we did. Interestingly, although they came from a large family of eight, only two of Joan's sisters had two children and the rest had only one each.

Our son Peter was born in Bishop Auckland in May 1960 and it was an easy birth. As I said earlier, in those days dads weren't allowed to see their babies being born, so I waited outside. Things have changed since then: my son has seen his children being born and so has my son-in-law. But not me. I do sometimes wish things had been different because now you see babies being born on the telly all the time and it looks like a wonderful and emotional experience.

My father idolized Dawn and Peter. He loved kids and used to visit quite often while we were posted home in Britain. He never came to Germany. Joan's parents did – we used to be able to get cheap tickets for direct family.

Four months after Peter was born, I was posted out to Hong Kong with the 14th Regiment Royal Artillery. I took the whole family. Peter was a baby so he doesn't remember any of it, but we sailed all the way there and the ship seemed to soothe him. Dawn was running about and had to go to school on the boat.

I remember the moment when we got to Colombo in Sri Lanka. We got to know a family on the journey who didn't want to go ashore so they agreed to look after Peter. Dawn has always been keen on animals, so we took some shore leave to take her to Colombo Zoo. She loved it. We took her to see a snake being fed a live rat and she couldn't believe her eyes as she stood there. She asked the zoo keeper about how long it would take to be crushed up inside. We thought she might cry at the sight of it, but she was mesmerized.

You have to barter a price with taxis in Colombo and you pay them upon the return trip as sometimes they had a tendency to take you and then not come back. I remember asking the driver how things were now with the British no longer there. He told me, 'I was waving the placard saying: "British go home", but now I'd like to amend that to "British come back".' I've seen that sort of reaction so many times.

We were posted to Hong Kong for three years, but we hadn't been there more than a year when I was summoned to the regimental office and told that the commanding officer wanted to see me. He told me that I had been marked absent.

'How do you mean?' I asked. 'From where?'

'The School of Artillery,' he said.

'I'm sorry, sir, you have to explain,' I replied.

'Do you remember the qualifying exam?' he asked.

I thought for a moment. 'Oh yes, I do,' I replied. 'I did it a year ago.'

'Did you know you had passed?' he asked.

'No,' I said. 'Well, no one's told me.'

It turned out that the bosses had written back to the school and said they wanted me on the next long gunnery service course. This was the senior course enabling attendees to learn the skills to teach the practice and science of artillery to junior members of the Royal Artillery.

'You're due to start your course next week, so you have to go home,' said the commanding officer. I was shocked. Our family had settled in Hong Kong and I didn't want to leave Joan and the children there alone, but duty called, so I was shipped out by the RAF, leaving Joan to follow a couple of weeks later. I'm so grateful I had friends in the mess who stepped in to help her pack and get her home. There was one problem, though: Joan had to get on a plane and she hated flying.

CHAPTER 26

Larkhill and the
Royal School of Artillery

I was settling into the School of Artillery in Larkhill when Joan joined me. It was her first flight and she had been frightened to death. She sat with Dawn on one side and Peter on the other and she said to herself that if the plane went down, they'd all go together. I felt awful for her having to travel alone, and I thought how brave she'd been.

After they landed safely, we went straight to my sister Maisie's wedding in London. Joan and the children had terrible jet lag, but someone close to Maisie realised they'd need to rest so offered them their flat to take it easy, then they could come to the wedding later.

I joined the course in Larkhill on Salisbury Plain and it was such hard work. Compared to others on the course, my lack of basic education was evident, so I had to work harder than most to catch up, while taking on the advanced gunnery knowledge at the same time. Joan was really supportive as I had to do so much homework to keep up. It was an uphill struggle but I was determined to do it and I had my wind beneath my wings supporting me all the way. I dedicate that song to Joan for a reason: whatever I did, she was there looking after me, willing me on.

At that point there was no married quarters available, so I found a cottage in a place called Durrington, near the kids' school, and settled them into the house until quarters were ready to move into. It was worth the wait. Our flash new quarters were these sturdy, modern buildings that were so smart. The whole family loved living there – Dawn went to school and joined the Brownies and Peter created havoc by running around everywhere. Joan quickly became known as 'Are you the lady who chases that young boy in the blue dungarees around the married quarters?'.

It was a happy time. We had a very nice Sergeants' Mess and, unlike before, I didn't have to do mess duty because I was one of the instructional staff. Although we'd settled into life there and although the course was supposed to be 14 months long, I found out I'd qualified a bit early. I was proud of this because it was such an intensive course that not everyone actually passed.

Towards the end of the course, three of us were called to the colonel's office on a Saturday morning, which normally means you're going to be told off for something. I was last in, wondering: What have I done? My dismay increased when the two other guys came out with long faces – they had been told to return to their unit because they weren't good enough.

Then I went in, and the colonel said, 'Now, I'm going to start by saying to the regimental sergeant major who has brought you in that this conversation never happened.' The sergeant major said, 'I don't know what you're talking about. What conversation?' By this time I was very confused and worried about what was coming next.

They told me was that I had received such good reports that I was going to be promoted to warrant officer – the promotion normally followed qualification from the course. But they could see, from Royal Artillery record, that I was already due for promotion because of my time served and my record. This was very good news. I couldn't be promoted while on the course, however, so I was given a choice of completing the course and then being promoted, or leaving the course without the qualification and being promoted straightaway.

'I can give you the option to go back to duty now and you'll be promoted within weeks,' said the colonel. 'Or, on the other hand – but I'm not saying this – it looks like you might be getting an appointment here at Larkhill. Now you won't know this until you finish the course. I'll give you until Monday to decide.'

But we were so happy there. 'I don't want to move my family,' I said. 'If I'm getting an appointment here, then I'll take that.'

And so I finished the course, pretending not to know that I had already passed and been offered a job instructing at Larkhill. I worked as hard as I ever had and got the cross gun barrels on my arm.

I was told I was being retained at officer's branch for another year and I'd be training young officers' gunnery, which was a feather in my cap. I was delighted to have been offered this job. These guys were straight from Sandhurst with their shiny pips on their shoulders. They had learned how to be officers and now they had to learn their trade. Gunnery is extremely difficult to teach, so I had to be systematic and disciplined. But we also had a lot of fun.

It was a good job and we were able to stay another year before being posted out to Germany again.

You still had to do your day job, but you also had to do range duties. You'd go out with the unit firing on the ranges and stay with them over the weekend. The first duty I was given was to accompany and instruct in gunnery the Honourable Artillery Company (HAC), who are a very elite Territorial Army unit, based in the City of London.

I duly reported to a grid reference on the firing range where I found a three-tonne truck that had been converted into the regimental field headquarters. Unlike other regiments, the HAC vehicle was beautifully appointed. I knocked on the door and this chap stuck his head out and said, 'Good day to you, Sergeant Major. Do come in. What will you have?' I was surprised to see they had a drinks cabinet. They were a lovely unit full of lawyers, insurance underwriters and stockbrokers, but they took their training very seriously. Often the senior men in their civilian lives would be junior to others within the regiment.

While at the gunnery school at Larkhill, my time was taken up with the young officers. There was so much to learn in the six months they were there, but they made sure they had their fun, especially on the final weekend, when they had their passing-out party. There is a huge Officers' Mess in Larkhill. As sergeant major, you'd be asked to go for dinner, but you would leave at a certain time because they were all going to get plastered. One morning, after a particularly messy final night, I was called, along with the two other warrant officer gunnery staff instructors, to see the school sergeant major.

We went straight to his office.

'Have you looked around the school?' he said.

'No, sir,' we replied, getting a bit worried.

'Will you look around the school?' he asked.

'Yes, sir,' we replied.

'Where were your officers last night?' he asked.

'They were partying last night,' I said, sheepishly.

'Yes,' he said. 'Go and see the results.'

We went to check. At the school there were many types of guns on display around the grounds. They were heavy and normally moved by vehicles – to move them by hand required significant teamwork. Now there were guns all over the place, even on the road. The young officers had obviously spent a good few hours, in the middle of the night, moving the guns all over the grounds of the school. I got the group together.

'Gentlemen, you've had your fun,' I said. 'The guns have to be replaced. No one wants to know who did it, so you need to take charge and have them all back by lunchtime.'

And they were.

CHAPTER 27

Canteens and camping

Joan and I loved our time in Germany, so I was pleased to be posted there again in 1963. I was posted to Hohne, which had a huge artillery firing range, sixty miles long and thirty miles wide. There was a small gunnery school and all summer we would go to the firing ranges with many other artillery units stationed across Germany. It was hard work. Sometimes, we would be up at the break of day and be away for 24 hours. It was live firing too, so you had to be extra careful about the range safety.

At first, Joan was happy about moving all the time, but then, having to find a new house and settle the family in became too much for her. All in all, Dawn went to 12 schools but she took it in her stride. Later, she went to art college and became a dress designer and now she teaches too. She's always found it easy to make friends, perhaps because she had to each time we moved to a new place. She and Peter were both very easy kids.

During the winter period in Germany, when we were running the courses, we got annoyed with the young officers and sergeants for dashing straight from their beds, skipping breakfast, to start the day's work at 9 o'clock. At the end of the first season, the colonel called us together and said, 'There is a problem. We're fed up with people turning up late and having had no breakfast. If you're in the Army and have to be somewhere at 9 o'clock, you damn well get there on time and make sure you're ready to start the day properly.'

Something had to be done. Because the men had had nothing to eat, they'd wait until breaktime at half ten, then hare off by car to the NAAFI, which was a short distance away, where they'd have their breakfast. It was so frustrating because a quarter-of-an-hour break would then take half an hour, so we had to find a way of stopping this. That's when we came up with the idea of running our own canteen at the base.

The colonel pointed out that the rules stated that we couldn't do this if we were less than a mile away from a NAAFI establishment. He said to me, 'Sergeant Major, why don't you do a survey to see how far our classroom is from the NAAFI?'

I decided to use my students to do a full ground survey to measure the exact distance from classroom to NAAFI. It was, in fact, 1.1 miles away, so we concluded that we *could* make our own canteen and we set it up in the attic of the gunnery school. We decided we would sell rolls, which we'd buy from the village, with ham and cheese for fillings. Then someone asked who would run it and Joan said she'd be up for doing it, along with a friend.

They did this every morning and it was so popular and the ladies sold so many rolls that they made quite a bit of money. The colonel became a little concerned as regulations were such that they shouldn't have been making significant sums. It was decided to use the money to buy camping equipment for the families of staff to use. We bought the very best equipment – two complete kits, with a trailer, tent and everything you need for a camping trip. During the summer months, these kits were well used by the staff. We loved camping when the kids were small and there was so much scope in Germany, so many places you could go.

The artillery school in Germany was next to a tank training establishment and there was a chap we knew who had a German wife and two small boys. When this guy met his wife, she couldn't speak English and, when the kids came along, she taught them French as well as German. When they chatted, they'd switch from one language to the other. He asked to borrow one of the camping kits, then asked me round one night to help him learn how to set up the tent. We put the frame up and threw on the canvas and it looked great. They were convinced they could do it, so off they went on leave.

When they got back, the chap said to me, 'Thanks for that. We had a wonderful holiday but it was a bit fraught on the first day.' They'd got to a campsite and his wife said she didn't like it, so they tried another and the same thing happened the next couple of times. By the fifth one, he put his foot down and put up the tent. He said it was a lovely campsite, surrounded by hedges, and his wife was very impressed. The chap sent his sons off to fill a rolling barrel up with water, so they trundled off and when they came back, they said, 'It's a funny place.'

'What do you mean?' he asked.

'No one has any clothes on,' one of them replied.

It turns out they were camping at a nudist colony. His wife said, 'I'm not coming out of this tent for the whole time we're here.'

The kids, on the other hand, stripped off and joined in.

He said the next morning, he went to the beach with the boys and he wore his trunks. But everyone else was running around starkers. To start with he was too embarrassed to look, but eventually he slipped his trunks off and lay on a towel. Once he realised no one was watching he played in the sand with the boys. When they got back to the tent, his wife was still refusing to come outside, but he worked on her and that evening he managed to get her to the beach. She was wearing a bikini, but he persuaded her to slip her top off. She took it in good humour, but it was another three days before she took the bottoms off. In the end, she loved it and he said that they were brown all over! They actually went back there the following summer.

CHAPTER 28

Leaving the Army

After four years in Germany, I went back home to England and on to Junior Leaders Regiment Royal Artillery in Bramcote Nuneaton, not far from Coventry. This is the modern equivalent of my Boys' Service – young men joining the Army under the age of 17 enter service in Junior Leaders as young recruits. There are not many of these junior regiments left across the British Army any more.

I took over from a colleague and, while we were based there, I had a responsibility for what we called the training brigade. We took the boys in, trained them and, after they had successfully passed out, they would then be sent to start their army life in regular units. I watched the first passing-out parade and it was lovely, but there were no artillery guns on parade on either side of the saluting base. I thought it would be a great idea to make two of the regimental guns fit for parade duty. There were forty guns in the unit, which were used for training purposes, but none of them were in a good enough condition to be used for parade duty.

My Aunty Maisie's husband Jack had an office in Leamington Spa. He worked as a tool controller for a big firm of engineers, so I asked him if we could get the guns repainted and all the brightwork polished. This was a significant task.

'How much will it cost?' I asked, thinking it would be a considerable sum.

'A bottle of wine,' he replied.

We had the guns painted and polished and they looked a treat. Jack had done me a huge favour. The colonel of the regiment was so delighted that we had improved the standards in the regiment.

I had 25 fantastic years in the Army, but I knew further progression would be difficult. Reluctantly Joan and I decided that our future would be better served if I retired from the Army while I was still young enough to build a life in civvy street. I could have done five more years, but I wanted to leave while young enough to start a second career. Joan was ready to settle down, too, so I put in for my discharge. It was a hard but rational decision to come out.

The Army changed me from a scruffy little urchin with no education to someone with a good standard of education and years of experience. Who knows where I would have ended up if I hadn't joined up? I'd have gone to Borstal or worse. The most important thing was, without the Army, I'd never have gone to Durham and met my Joan. She had been a wonderful army wife, but she was getting fed up with the constant relocation.

Joan changed my life. She gave me stability. She came from a secure background and a good family. I was strong, but she was tough in a different way. She never shouted at anybody, but she got things done.

When I was on my long gunnery course, she was very supportive and she kept gently pushing. I really needed Joan there to help me get through it. By the end of that course, Joan knew almost as much as I did about gunnery!

The secret to a long marriage is tolerance. Joan and I matured into grown-up parenthood together. I was fortunate in life that at times when so many marriages go wrong, mine was good and firm.

The Army had been such a big part of my life so, even though I knew the time was right, I was still slightly reluctant to leave. On my last morning at Junior Leaders, I was in my office. A fun-loving staff sergeant working for me suddenly locked the door from the outside and put a sheet of paper over the window. I was locked in and effectively blind. 'What are you doing?' I shouted. 'I'll put you on a charge!' 'I'm sorry,' he said. 'Orders is orders.'

I wondered what was going on, then I heard the whole regiment being marched into the gunnery school hangar. The staff sergeant told me to come out as the colonel was there and wanted to talk to me. I put my cap and belt on and was released from the room.

I was most surprised to see the colonel and the whole regiment were all on parade to give me a send-off. The colonel made a very kind and glowing speech, which was lovely to hear, and I was presented with a shell case and a gun rammer inscribed with my service record. I still have them today in my room at the Royal Hospital Chelsea.

At that point I wondered: Have I done the right thing? I was about to enter a whole different world.

PART 7

Life after
the Army

CHAPTER 29

Civvy street

I'd done it. I had retired from the Army. It was 1970 and, although I had completed 25 years in the Royal Artillery, as I had joined when I was so young I was now only forty years old. I was now having to plan a new life in civvy street with Joan. What more did I need? Well, I suppose a job might come in handy as we still had to make ends meet. Luckily for me, I had my good friend Ken Brown, my old mate from Brancepeth, Korea and Hong Kong.

Back then, the pair of us were as thick as thieves when we were touring with the concert party and posted to Hong Kong. But when he left for Australia to marry his sweetheart, who was also called Joan (it was a popular name back then!), we didn't see him again and only received the odd correspondence from him.

When Ken touched down in Oz, he certainly didn't let the grass grow under his feet. He had gone on to become a successful salesman. It was hardly a surprise because, as a natural-born comedian, Ken could talk the hind legs off a donkey and have people eating out of his hand. It seemed that the rather untamed sense of humour the commanding officer at Brancepeth had tried to knock out of him actually had worked in his favour as he had ended up making a good living for himself by working his way up the ladder at the confectionery company Nestlé in Australia. However, after a few years of raking it in and having a couple of kids, he and Joan decided to return home to the UK. Using the amazing reputation he had built up at Nestlé in Australia, he managed to obtain another good position at the same company in the UK and settled in Surrey.

Once he got his bearings, my ambitious friend decided to branch out on his own and launched his own business producing products for vending machines, which again he turned into a massive success.

That's when he first got in touch with me. I was doing that long course at the Royal School of Artillery in Larkhill in Wiltshire at the time and a big brown envelope was delivered to me from Royal Artillery Records labelled 'Please find enclosed a letter from a Mr Brown'. (Post addressed to us would be sent via the records department.) He said he wanted to come and see me because he had a proposition that might interest me, which naturally intrigued me. I knew Ken was very successful and I assumed he was thinking about asking me to work with him. I was touched by this. He really did look after his mates, did Ken. In normal circumstances, I would have seriously considered what he was offering but, as I was slap, bang, wallop in the middle of a massive course, I knew I probably wouldn't have time to commit. It had been years since we'd properly seen each other, however, so I invited Ken up to see us for a catch-up. I remember, as Joan and I were preparing for his arrival, we both had a laugh about how we thought he would arrive. Would he be a wind-up merchant and drive up in a dodgy old van or would he be lording it in a Roller? As it turned out, he opted for the Rolls-Royce. Can you believe it? You had to give it to the fella – the boy had done good and he did it off his own back. It just goes to show you that sometimes the fellas who need 'smartening up' are just fine the way they are.

It was great to see Ken. He looked the same, only richer. Just as I thought, Ken had come to ask me if I would consider working with him at some point in the future. I explained to him that I intended to stay for the moment, but I knew I would move on in about four or five years. Ken said he would wait and uttered the magic words, 'If you are ever looking for a job, I'll make sure you get one. And it will be a good one.'

And so it was. Ken stuck to his word, God love him, and that's exactly what happened. When I left the Army, I got in touch with him and he made me a development manager, selling products for vending machines. Of course, I had no experience whatsoever in this field, but Ken believed in me and chucked me in at the deep end. We'd worked together long enough for him to know that I was a fast learner and could get any job done, which I greatly appreciated.

Things were looking up, all of a sudden. I had a job, money was coming in and we were able to buy our first-ever civilian house. It was just an ordinary semi in Thorpe St Andrew, Norwich, but it was ours and that felt great. It had a lovely garden, which Joan really took care of, and even though I was nowhere near as green-fingered as she was, that didn't stop her from setting me tasks – she proved to be a very able foreman.

On the surface, life was going well. But what I hadn't anticipated was that the change in lifestyle would be hard for me to come to terms with. Before I'd quit, I had been excited about having a different pace of life and spending more time with Joan. But, for the first few months, it was a really unhappy time for me. I didn't know what I was doing and I didn't find living in Norwich easy. Everything was different. It was hard to settle into the 'real' world. Working at Ken's factory was definitely a good move, but I was learning my trade on the job, so wasn't feeling on top of everything the way I normally would be. It started to dawn on me that there were certain things that you can't do in civvy street that you did in the Army because everything in life costs money. I had left a situation where everything was done for me, where I didn't have to worry about finding a job because I was posted from place to place, where I didn't have to worry about finding somewhere to live, I simply moved into married quarters. And then there were the bills and rates. I really hadn't appreciated how much stuff was done for us in the Army.

On top of that, I didn't understand what people were talking about half the time. It felt like I spoke a different language as we had our own way of talking in the Army. As a result, I became really depressed – I felt like a fish out of water.

One day, for example, I received a card in a manila envelope, which had a lot of squares on it. I had no idea what it meant and innocently said to Joan, 'What on earth is this for?'

She looked at me as if I had just asked her what a Christmas tree was. 'Are you taking the mickey, Hunk?' she laughed.

I shook my head, confused. 'Darling, I don't have the foggiest idea what this is.' When she realised that I genuinely didn't know what it meant, she gave me a warm, understanding smile and told me they were my 'cards'.

In those days, your National Insurance stamps were called 'cards' – hence that popular expression, 'you got your cards', when you were let go from a job. I couldn't believe I was so naïve about life. I was forty years old, with a wife and kids, and I didn't know what this piece of paper was. This made me feel very unsure of myself.

I was not in a good way. I felt I didn't fit in. I didn't understand what was going on. Luckily for me, Joan was a canny lass, noticed the change in me and realised that I wasn't coping very well. I was getting grumpy, was short with her and I was much more reticent than normal. But she dealt with it in her own way. Looking back, I feel really sorry for her because she was having to deal with a husband who was in a depressed state, who didn't know what the hell what was happening. But she put up with me and made sure my state of mind didn't get worse, and if it hadn't been for her stoicism I don't know what would have happened.

I continued to work with Ken for a couple of years in all, until he decided he wanted to combine several of his companies into just one. This would mean that he would need to find a property that would be able to contain them all under one roof. He asked me to help him hunt down a suitable factory at a farm address in Hampshire. Heading down to the Wallops in Hampshire, I did a recce and stumbled upon a redundant turkey farm that was comprised of all these amazing buildings. The main office building looked like a big house. It had Ken written all over it. I told him he had to come down straightaway to check it out. He did, fell in love with it and made an offer immediately, knocking five-thousand pounds off the asking price in the process.

Ken was impressed that I was able to get things done fast so he asked me if I could oversee the various companies that would be moving into the site, which I agreed to. Once that mission was accomplished, Ken took me to one side and asked, 'So, Colin, when are you moving down, then?'

I was confused. 'Down where?'

Ken laughed. 'Down here, of course. You've set everything up so you might as well come and work here too.' He looked me in the eye, sensing I wasn't biting. 'I will make it worth your while.'

The offer was tempting and I was very pleased that Ken saw me as a key member of his team, but I had to think about the bigger picture. I had to think about Joan and the new life we had set up in Norwich.

'Look, Ken,' I said, nervously. 'You've given me so many opportunities already and I really would love to stay with you because you are my oldest friend, but I can't. Joan doesn't want to move any more. We've moved around so much and we've finally found a place to settle.'

What I told him was true, but there were other reasons I didn't want to uproot the family again. Dawn had been to more than 12 schools since she was born and Peter was a little behind with his reading, which was a bit worrying, but we put it down to the fact that we were moving around so often. We eventually found another school for Peter and he improved very quickly.

We loved our house very much and we lived there for forty years. In spite of my initial doubts, I grew to love Norwich a lot and it became our home. It was such a lovely place to live. We lived on the eastern side of the city on an estate that was on the edge of farmland with woods. Joan and I would venture out for walks all the time, it was so invigorating. I wish I could do it now, but I don't have the breath and my legs won't carry me.

Eventually, Dawn went off to college to study fashion design, leaving just three of us. It was tough to lose Dawn to the real world, but we understood this was a rite of passage and we got used to it. Luckily, we still had Peter to dote on and we had a great time as a family and would go off on camping holidays. Sometimes Peter and I would go fishing. He loved to fish and he was good at it. We got up to so much. Norfolk was great for doing stuff outside and of course it was great for music. But more on that later.

After I turned Ken down, I went from one job to the next for a time. I worked on a building site to keep myself busy and to earn money. I tried working for the NHS. The job was okay, but the wages weren't very good. Then I saw an advert for the Agricultural Training Board – the word 'training' obviously got me excited so I spent the next few years working there. It paid the bills, but it could never excite me the way the Army did.

One Christmas, Joan and I were invited along to one of my regimental association dinners. It was lovely to catch up with various old faces and chat about the old days. When we sat down for dinner, I ended up sitting next to Alan Griffiths, this rather charismatic chap who was the treasurer of the association. During the evening, two singers – a tenor and a soprano – performed some musical theatre songs, which had me moving around in my seat. The fellow next to me noticed. 'So you like music?' he said enthusiastically.

'I love music,' I replied. 'I love listening to it and I love performing it too.'

He narrowed his eyes with interest. 'Ah, so you sing?'

'I do,' I answered hesitantly, wondering where this chap was headed with this.

He leaned in a little closer, as if about to share a wicked secret. 'These two performers are members of the operatic society, the Norfolk Opera Players, that I'm part of.' I could see he was trying to gauge what I was thinking. 'Would you be interested?'

'Interested in what?' I ventured, still no clearer about what he was asking.

'We are rehearsing *Carmen* at the Theatre Royal at the moment,' he laughed, swigging his drink. 'There are about sixty of us. We are looking for someone to join the chorus and teach the soldiers to use swords and march for a scene in which the corporal falls in love with Carmen. How does that sound?'

I was bursting with joy. The chance to sing on stage and relive my military past – what more could I ask for? 'That's a piece of cake,' I smiled.

A couple of days later, I started as a Norfolk Opera Player. It was a renowned theatrical company that had been founded by Robert and Audrey Yates a few years prior. He was a semi-professional bass and she was a contralto. They were lovely people and they took their shows very seriously. Audrey would later launch a ladies-only choir called Wings of Song, which Joan would subsequently join. My role was two-fold. One was to learn the chorus parts and the other to teach the men playing the soldiers how to march and hold a sword.

I soon discovered, however, that these actor types were not the easiest to work with. One thespian, a little Italian chap, had a problem holding his sword – he insisted on clutching it in his left hand.

'But I'm left-handed,' he pleaded when I told him he had to swap hands for the scene. 'I'm left-handed,' he repeated, ignoring what I was saying.

I said to him slowly and firmly, just as I would have to any disobedient young soldier, 'I don't care. You would fight with your left hand, but for drill purposes we all have to be the same. You have to use your right hand.'

He muttered something in Italian but then reluctantly took orders!

I loved the experience. I felt like I was back in the Army. I really got into the role and I would sometimes shout at them too. They must have thought, 'Who is he?'

Seeing how much fun I was having with the Players, Joan started to show an interest in the them too. Although the pair of us would sing and dance around the house all the time, performing wasn't her initial interest. She had her eye on the wardrobe department.

When we started work on *Prince Igor*, she became a props mistress and, like everything Joan did, she did it extremely well. She ensured the production had all the necessary props for the show, which was a tough task because the budget was very small indeed. But Joan always had a head full of ideas and would dream up a way of making something, especially if it was something made of fabric. If she needed things made from wood, I'd come in very handy indeed. There was also a self-employed builder who made the special swords that had to be blunted so they didn't hurt anyone.

A while later, Richard White, a guest director who went on to become a very good friend, produced two Gilbert and Sullivan operas, *The Mikado* and *The Yeoman of the Guard*. In the latter, Joan and I got to dance on stage. Richard didn't only like the orchestra playing the prelude, he also wanted the stage to be filled, so he had the pair of us and some other cast members performing a dance. I also played the Lieutenant of the Tower in the show, so had to hastily dash off stage, stick on a false moustache and a beard and don another costume. This production started off our musical career, which would carry on for many years.

What we loved about being part of the Players was that we were performing a different type of music to what we were used to singing. We'd only ever sung swing numbers before so this really pushed us and made it a lot more fun. We even took singing lessons so we could project the right way! The Players became a bit of a way of life for us and we even roped Peter into a couple of the operas. He didn't have much of a voice, bless him, but he threw himself into it and loved to act. In fact, he used to chuck himself into the action and get a little too carried away! In one opera, there was a scene where the soldiers are fighting with metal swords. Normally, actors will *pretend* to whack each other with their weapons, but Peter was very enthusiastic – too enthusiastic – and started whacking me with it. Needless to say, he loved having a go, even if he was not destined for a life on the stage.

We stayed with the Norfolk Operatic Players for 25 wonderful years, enjoying every moment of the musical madness. Joan took on various singing roles, as well as fulfilling her dream of becoming wardrobe mistress, while I became vice chairman of the society.

CHAPTER 30

Time to slow down

There comes a time in your life when you know it's time to slow things down and start to appreciate the life you have left. Joan and I were lucky. We had had an active and fruitful life but it had shot by so quickly that we weren't really able to take a moment to step back and take it all in. But now, in our mid-sixties, we both realised it was time to enjoy some much-needed quality time together.

Looking back, it was like our lives had been on fast forward. My courtship with Joan had been a magical whirlwind that came out of nowhere but gave me my first taste of responsibility and stability. I was then whisked away to the Korean War for two years, at a time when Joan and I should have been getting to know each other better and making the silly mistakes young couples do. But while many military couples around me had relationships that were falling apart, I was incredibly lucky to have an amazing, loyal and supportive wife like Joan, who was constantly there for me. She could have quite easily given up on me, moved on, and found someone else but she didn't. Instead she stuck by me and accompanied me around the world while I carried out my military duties. She never complained once about the constant upheaval she endured. She would always tell me that as long as we were together, she'd be happy. And we were. For almost fifty years we had barely spent a night apart and very rarely argued. I was the luckiest man alive. And now, in 1995, we felt we were finally ready to put work and distractions behind us and enjoy the kind of life we'd always wanted to have before it was too late. We were lucky because at this stage in our lives we were in a good position to do so. We didn't need lots of things. We had a nice little nest egg in the bank, we had our house and our kids were all grown-up and didn't need us as they used to.

Dawn had gone to London because there wasn't much opportunity for a dress designer in Norwich, while Peter went to university and then on to a career in the computer industry. I was pleased to see that neither of them flitted from job to job. They had stability, which I think they got from their mother. We were very happy when Dawn introduced us to her Lebanese boyfriend, Wajdi – we liked him from the start. If he and Dawn were coming up for the weekend, he would ring Joan and request an 'English dinner'. After they married, Dawn and Wajdi settled in North London and, a few years later, announced that Dawn was pregnant. I was going to be a grandad! Joan and I were both overjoyed. Ashley was born and Alice followed four years later. Joan often went down to London to see the girls and, when they were older, they came to us in Norwich. Peter went on to marry a wonderful girl called Sue and two more grandchilden followed – Charlotte (known by her middle name, Honey) and Oliver (known as Ollie). But I am getting ahead of myself here.

Now it was our time, a time to enjoy a proper life together, not just snatches of conversation here and there after a hard day at work. We wanted to do the things that made us happy and no longer have to think about pleasing anyone else. That's the best thing about retirement. No one is relying on you. You make your own decisions, at your own pace.

Joan and I used to find a lot of pleasure in many things. We were avid readers, we liked attending the odd lecture at the local hall and Joan enjoyed pottering around in the garden. She still loved fashion and beauty and was always well turned out, dressed in classic, sophisticated garments, her face beautifully made up.

Joan and I weren't, therefore, the kind of folks to sit around and do nothing. We wanted to keep our minds alive and so we kept ourselves physically active. We'd go for long walks around the area and into the local fields and woods, which we loved, and we attended our local gym two or three times a week, where we'd spend an hour working out, before a well-deserved sit-down, reading the newspapers with a coffee.

Music was still a massively important part of our lives and we still had a great deal of fun and fulfilment working with the Norfolk Opera Players. But that wasn't enough for us. Joan and I were members of a small singing group and toured the local area performing songs at old people's homes, clubs and The Big C Centre, a wonderful support centre helping people living with cancer. It was heartwarming being able to make a difference to the lives of those who were going through a tough time.

We were very rarely apart, unless Joan was attending rehearsals for her ladies' choir meetings, or if I was invited along to a regimental association get-together or function held by the Rotary Club of which I was a member. Joan hadn't joined the ladies equivalent of these organizations but thoroughly enjoyed accompanying me. She was the perfect party guest – she always looked good and would talk at length to absolutely anyone. Sometimes, when she was in full swing, I would simply stare at her in awe as she charmed whoever had the fortune of crossing her path. That was my Joan and I loved her for it.

Retirement was working for us. We had all the time in the world to do as we pleased and, as a result, we felt more spritely and mentally stimulated than we ever had. But while we seemed to be the masters of our day-to-day lives, the one thing we didn't have any control over was what was going on inside of us. It's a sad but inevitable rite of passage that as we get older, our bodies will get weaker and ultimately become more vunerable. That's just the way it goes, I'm afraid. Of course, there are perhaps ways of delaying the process by keeping our bodies in tip-top shape which, in fairness, is what Joan and I did, and partly explains how I've made it to 89 years old, but unfortunately we cannot control what nature decrees.

It was some time earlier, when I was 62 and still working, when I had my first heart attack. It frightened the bloody life out of me, let me tell you, but it didn't beat me. I had been having chest pains for some time but had put them down to indigestion, as we all tend to. Never one to let a silly pain get the better of me, I bull-headedly continued to attend the gym, sing and swim, and thought nothing more of it. However, it all came to a head when Joan and I went to visit the family in London for Christmas in 1992.

After spending Christmas Day at Dawn's, the whole family moved on to spend Boxing Day at Peter's flat in Blackheath. After lunch, Ashley, who was four at the time, was very keen to visit a traditional funfair on the local common. I love kids and there is no time of year that's more exciting for them than the festive period, so to watch Ashley skipping gaily along the road, excited about going to the fair, was a joy to behold. This is what being a kid is all about. As we turned a corner, the colourful flashing lights of the fair came into view and Ashley started giddily jumping up and down on the spot, grabbing my hand and pulling me along the road towards it. Because I was still feeling pains in my chest, which I was trying to keep myself, I encouraged Ashley to slow down a little.

Once we'd reached the fair, Ashley's eyes were as large as saucers as she took in the attractions, like the giant Ferris wheel, the dodgems, the waltzers and the carousel, all of which were decked out in bright, colourful bulbs that disguised the jaded and cracked paintwork. But what appeared to mesmerize Ashley most of all was the big red-and-white-striped helter-skelter that towered above us. 'I want to go, I want to go,' Ashley pleaded, dragging me by the hand. The pain in my chest was fierce by now and I was finding it hard to stand on two feet, but I couldn't resist my excited little granddaughter and agreed to accompany her up what seemed like hundreds of steps. Big mistake. By the time, we reached the top, I was breathless and in a lot of pain, but somehow Ashley's carefree and innocent exuberance took my mind off the pain. Grabbing our wicker mats, I helped Ashley aboard, then gave her a gentle push and watched her whoosh away down the spiral slide out of sight, screaming gleefully as she went. I climbed on and followed her at top speed. The journey was short but the pains in my chest meant I couldn't enjoy the exhilarating ride and, as I approached the end of the slide and bounced onto the soft mat at the bottom, it felt for one terrifying moment as if I were whooshing towards the light. As I regained my composure, Ashley was jumping up and down, squealing, 'Again, again!'

I remained in pain that night on the drive back from London to Norwich, but I didn't let on to anyone and tried to push it to the back of my mind. The next morning, back in Norwich, when I accompanied Joan to the shops to exchange a gift, the throbbing pain was becoming unbearable. Instead of joining her in the shop, I told Joan I'd stay in the car as I was feeling a little jaded, but when she got back she was concerned to see that I had taken my coat off and was sweating profusely. She could tell immediately that something was wrong and I explained that I had been experiencing chest pains for some time. 'You're so daft,' she snapped. 'You should have said.' Moving me over to the passenger seat, she jumped behind the wheel and tore off to the surgery. When we got there, she rushed inside and practically dragged the doctor out to the street to examine me with his ECG machine in tow. All of a sudden, an ambulance rolled up beside us, which the doctor had already called for, and I suddenly became nervous, aware that I had no control over what my body was doing to me.

The ambulance roared through the streets of Norwich with its blues and twos blasting. I started to worry.

'Am I dying?' I asked, wondering why we were in such a hurry.

'No, no,' the paramedic replied calmly, 'we're just trying to get through the traffic.'

As we bumped and bounced our way across the city, it dawned on me for the first time that perhaps I was actually having a heart attack. I had all the typical symptoms, including that tight band-like feeling across the chest. I don't know why I hadn't thought of it before!

I got rushed into a booth where medics set about examining me. I have to confess, I was quite scared because I really didn't know what was going on or if I would make it through. I was also upset because I could see that Joan was very concerned and the last thing I wanted was for her to worry about me. Luckily, an insightful young male nurse noticed Joan's worry and led her away to a room, got her a cup of tea and calmed her down while the doctors set to work on me.

By the time she came back I was wired up to all sorts of machines. Although I was stable, they wanted to keep me overnight. They warned me to be more careful in future about what I was doing. 'If you feel what could be an angina pain, just stop what you are doing,' the doctor told me. Of course, I hadn't stopped at the time and had just kept going in spite of the pain. But this heart attack was a pretty scary wake-up call because I started to think about all the things I actually could have lost – like Joan – so I decided it was time to look after myself more.

But even though I was more careful about my health, that didn't stop me from having a second blasted heart attack shortly afterwards. This time the doctor decided that I needed stents, which are placed into the vein to expand them, and I had three of them fitted, one in the middle of my chest and two in the upper part of my heart.

Thankfully, that did the trick and I was fast on the mend. But little did Joan or I know that there was a dark shadow waiting in the wings that would rip our world apart.

CHAPTER 31

Courage and strength

'I've found a lump in my breast,' Joan told me matter-of-factly one day in 2009.

I was reading the newspaper in my armchair when she strolled into the living room and rather casually dropped her bombshell.

'Are you sure?' I asked redundantly, trying to stall for time so that I could get my head around what she had just told me. I was immediately thinking the worst, as we all do, but I didn't want to react in a way that would put her on edge.

'Yes, one hundred per cent sure,' she replied. 'I've already made an appointment with the doctor to get it seen to. Fancy a cup of tea?'

That was my Joan, taking everything in her stride, but so began a rollercoaster journey that would ultimately put the two of us to the test and lead to the darkest time of my life.

Joan never looked her age. It must have been the way we led our lives, but folks were constantly surprised that she was a year shy of eighty. Joan had been right about the lump and was diagnosed with breast cancer shortly afterwards. Cancer is a horrid word. The minute you hear it, you can't help but think the worst, even though so many people these days pull through. But to Joan's credit, when she was told the news, she was very stoic and took it on the chin, way better than I ever would. I was sad and angry and heartbroken, but of course I could never let on to Joan. She didn't need me breaking down when she needed strength around her.

We went back to the hospital to find out how the doctor wanted to proceed with treatment. We brought our two best friends, Annette and Susie, along for moral support. They waited patiently outside the room while Joan and I were told what course of action would be taken.

The doctor explained that the cancer was just in the breast and that it didn't look like it had spread anywhere else. He felt the best action would be to perform a mastectomy, which we both agreed with. We were then passed on to a nurse who took us to another room to explain what the procedure would involve. All the way through the conversation, I noticed that the nurse kept looking at me intently and I couldn't work out why.

Afterwards, I told Annette and Susie about the nurse's watchful gaze and Annette, who was a retired medic, said to me, 'Of course she was staring at you. Joan's having a mastectomy. In some cases, men have felt their wives are disfigured and less attractive after the operation. We know it won't affect you but that's what she's worrying about, because a lot of men have rejected their wives.' I was stunned. How could any man consider his wife disfigured when her mastectomy is saving her life? All I wanted was for my wife to be well again. If a mastectomy ensured her good health, then so be it.

When we got home, we talked it over and I was surprised and heartbroken to hear Joan admit to me that she was upset that the operation would leave her 'disfigured' and was worried about the effect it would have on me. I told her if it meant the cancer was gone, I would not be worried about the way she looked in the slightest. 'I want you to be better again,' I said to her. 'You'll still be the same person. Losing a breast won't change who you are, Joan. It won't change the way I feel for you. I will love you just the same.'

Throughout this time, Joan remained very stoic. She might have been boiling on the inside but she didn't ever show it. She was tough and adamant that she would battle through it the best she could and come out the other side feeling stronger than ever.

When it came to the procedure itself, Joan faced it with typical courage and strength, just as I expected her to. She was braver than me, that's for sure. While she was in theatre, I worried like mad about what might happen, even though I knew she'd be fine. But, in these situations, it's hard not to think about every single possible scenario that could arise and, of course, the idea of losing Joan occasionally ran through my mind. But I wasn't going to let that happen. Joan was going to beat this terrible disease. If anything, I'd probably go first. That's the way I wanted it.

After the operation, the doctors had some good news for us. Worries that the cancer may have spread to the lymph nodes proved needless and the mastectomy meant that she was now cancer-free. The words were like music to my ears and you could see utter relief on Joan's beautiful face.

As with every cancer patient who is given the all clear, Joan was told she would have to have an annual check-up for the next five years to see whether the cancer had returned. Each time the doctor happily told us that there wasn't any sign of it. Joan was fighting fit and we were thrilled.

In 2014 we hoped we'd reached the all-important fifth year of clear check-up results. If she got the all clear again, Joan would no longer need regular check-ups, which would be a welcome relief. It was a tense day, to say the least, as that day's feedback could change our lives. The surgeon called us into the room and sat us down. To start with, I wasn't sure what the doctor was going to say as he looked pretty sombre as doctors sometimes are. But then he smiled and said, 'I don't think I have to see you any more.' The spectre of cancer was no longer there. Joan had beaten the cancer into touch. Now she was out of the darkness and we could finally step into the light again and live happily ever after.

Or so we thought.

CHAPTER 32

Heartbreak

For the next two years, Joan and I lived life to the full. We'd both experienced frightening health issues that could have easily spelled the end, but we felt like we'd been given a second chance. We felt invincible. We were well into our eighties by now, but we were still as fit as fiddles and full of optimism. We threw ourselves into everything we did and we felt like the world was ours.

Two years later, fate dealt us a cruel card. The cancer was back again and this time the prognosis wasn't good.

I can't remember exactly how Joan knew something was wrong on this occasion. I think she had been suffering pains and was feeling exhausted all the time. She went to the doctor who carried out some tests and then we waited. The results were like a body blow – the cancer was in her lungs. The doctor explained that they were the same cells that had attacked her before and had probably been lying dormant for years. We were devastated.

'What can we do?' I asked, desperate to know what action the medics were planning to take. Their answer wasn't one I was prepared for or wanted to hear.

'There's nothing we can do to get rid of the cancer,' the doctor said. 'But we can prolong life using various methods.'

I couldn't really believe what I was hearing. I couldn't lose Joan, I was nothing without her. There must be something that could be done, surely! I pleaded, but the doctor could offer no satisfactory response.

While I was losing my mind with worry and sadness, Joan sat beside me, typically calm and stoic, nodding and taking in all the information very matter-of-factly. That was Joan.

Joan had treatment to make her life comfortable, but she said she wanted to live her remaining days at home with me, watching *Loose Women* on the telly, and singing and dancing around the living room when the mood took her. I didn't argue, even though I wanted to try to convince her to fight this horrible disease.

In the end, I had to accept that I was going to lose her. It took a while for it to sink in that there was nothing I or anyone could do to help her. It was so unfair. What had she done to deserve this death sentence? She was a good and caring woman. It just felt cruel to take away a life from someone who deserved to live a long and happy one.

To look at her you'd never know she had cancer. She looked so healthy, so alive, that on occasion I did wonder if the doctors had got it all wrong. In spite of her illness, Joan carried on as if she was fit and healthy, always dressing immaculately and putting on her make-up. She loved dressing up and going out, so we'd make the effort to go to fancy places so she had a reason to look glamorous.

Although, in general, we had never shied away from talking about tough subjects, we both chose not to speak about 'the end', whenever that would be. It was the one thing we didn't like to think about.

Avoiding it made it seem less real. I felt that if you didn't talk about it, it might just go away. If only it were that easy.

The only time cancer was ever discussed was when we had to go The Big C Centre across town for Joan's weekly appointment. She would see a little Sri Lankan doctor, who was about the same size as Joan, and he would check how she was doing and drain a litre of fluid from her lungs. I'd sit there in silence, just holding her hand tightly.

The funny thing is, The Big C was one of the many places Joan and I used to sing at to raise funds for its upkeep. To think that we were now coming to the centre for our own very personal reason was sadly ironic.

The medics and patients at the centre couldn't believe that Joan was the one who was ill because she looked so well. They always thought she was there supporting a loved one who was going through the throes of cancer. But then I started to notice that she wasn't eating and that she was losing considerable amounts of weight.

I was very determined that Joan eat, but she said she couldn't stomach food and that upset me. I used to say to her, 'If you don't eat, you'll get weak.' But she never listened to me. It's funny, when she was young she loved eating chip butties. She'd eat lots of them, but never seemed to put on an ounce of weight. I always used to say she was seven stone wet through.

It was during one of our visits to the The Big C that I met a young woman who was looking after her poorly sister-in-law. We got talking about our situations and she mentioned that her relative hadn't been eating for a while. When I said Joan was finding it hard too and that I was worrying myself silly, she suggested that I try preparing for her some mashed avocado on toast, sprinkled with salt and pepper. When we got home, I did just that and Joan loved it.

Aside from her weight loss, Joan continued to show no real signs of illness as time went on, so we never really knew when the end might be, which was good, I think. Every week she would visit our friend Susie's reflexology clinic. Joan really enjoyed her sessions and she'd come home feeling much calmer. I think these natural treatments ensured that she was living relatively pain-free.

One afternoon, while I was busy in the kitchen preparing a baked potato with cheese and beans for lunch for the two of us, Joan was in the other room settling herself into her armchair to watch her favourite TV show, *Loose Women*. She loved the girls and always referred to them as the 'Naughty Girls' because they were so outrageously open and honest about their personal lives, but her absolute favourite was Ruth Langsford. 'Oh, she's such a nice woman! I don't know how she puts up with that Eamonn!' she'd say, referring to Ruth's TV presenter husband.

As I brought her lunch through to the sitting room, Joan enthusiastically listed which of the women were on today's panel. Ruth, sadly, wasn't among them, but she was still excited to hear what Nadia Sawalha and Coleen Nolan had to say about what was happening in the news that day. I put her lunch on one of those trays that you can place over someone's lap, retreated to my own seat by the window and hungrily dug into my baked potato.

Joan suddenly called out my name and I froze. There was something about the way she said it that sounded unusual and

I knew instantly that she was dying. Don't ask me how I knew, I just did. I guess we had been together so long, we'd become almost one person. And I could sense something was wrong. I knew this was it. I could tell from the way she said my name.

I looked over at her. The colour in her face had gone, she looked almost ghostly. I dashed to her and, as soon as I took the tray away, she collapsed into my arms. Carefully I eased her down onto the floor, she looked peaceful and thankfully didn't appear to be in pain.

I called for an ambulance straightaway, but the woman on the other end of the line had all those questions they always ask. 'Just get an ambulance here now!' I barked.

While I waited for the medics to arrive I started performing CPR on Joan, which I used to teach back in the Army, and prayed that this wasn't the end. However, I knew deep down that she wasn't going to make it. I think her heart had already stopped. But I didn't dare stop, just in case there was a chance of keeping her alive.

When the ambulance finally arrived, the paramedic could see that I was trying to keep her alive and told me to carry on while he went to fetch his kit. When he returned, he took over and told me to sit in the kitchen. A female member of the crew sat with me and made me a cup of tea and asked me all about Joan and how long we had been together. She was a lovely girl, softly spoken and kind, and she tried to give me hope, telling me that her colleague was trying everything he could to make her better. But I told her I knew it was too late.

Moments later, the first paramedic joined us to confirm that Joan had indeed died. Even though I had expected it, hearing it out loud hit me hard. I tried to keep a stiff upper lip, but I just couldn't do it.

Because her death was classed as a sudden death, the police were required to call round. The young constable who turned up was such a sweet and kind young man, just like the paramedics had been, and helped make this terrible situation easier to deal with. (I later wrote to the ambulance depot and the chief constable to praise them for how they had treated me.)

The paramedics told me they were ready to take Joan away and asked me if I'd like to say any last words to her. Of course I couldn't let them take her away without me seeing her. When I was alone, I knelt beside her and held her hand in mine. It was still warm. I looked at her. She was still beautiful and it looked like she was sleeping. I whispered to her how much I loved her and how hard life was going to be without her. I promised her that I would get hold of Dawn and Peter to let them know what was going on as soon as possible. Then I kissed her gently on the forehead and said my last goodbye to the woman I had shared 66 years of my life with.

I couldn't bring myself to watch as they took Joan away. Instead I sat in the kitchen going over what had happened that afternoon. I was absolutely destroyed. My wife, the woman I loved and had spent almost every day of my life with, was gone and she wasn't coming back. I couldn't quite get my head around that. The one blessing was that it appeared that Joan had endured a fast and painless death, which I dare say was the way she would have wanted to go.

As I waited for Peter and Dawn to join me, I started to think about what happens when someone dies. I'm not deeply religious so I'm not sure if I actually believe there is another life. Not even the cleverest scientists know what lies beyond death. But Joan does, because if there is another place we go to, then she's there already, waiting. So, maybe one day, we will meet again.

CHAPTER 33

Saying goodbye

Joan died five days before Christmas and I knew one thing for sure – she would have hated it if Christmas was overshadowed by sadness. I said to Peter and Dawn that we had to make sure that we try to celebrate it just like any other year. Towards the end of the day, we were all sitting in the kitchen and I found myself singing what the family affectionately refer to as 'Mum's song' – 'Wind Beneath My Wings'. We all ended up in floods of tears, toasting Joan/Mum/ Grandma, wondering how we would ever survive without her.

I'd also come to another decision. Once Christmas was over and Joan had been laid to rest in January, I would close up the house and move away. The idea of rattling around the house with all those pictures of Joan and all the memories of our time together in the house was simply too much to bear. Every time I passed her empty armchair, it just broke my heart! When certain songs came on the radio, I'd think back to the times we'd danced to it in the living room. The house was haunted with so many memories that I needed to break free so that I wasn't living in constant heartbreak.

Besides, the house was way too big for a little old man like me. What did I need with a three-bedroom house all to myself? When I told the kids about my plans to sell the family home, they understood completely and Peter asked if I planned to do what I'd said I'd do a couple of years before – apply to live in at the Royal Hospital Chelsea.

A couple of Christmases before, I'd come across an advert that said 'retire in style' at the Royal Hospital. I thought at the time that it might actually be a good idea in the very unlikely event that Joan were to pass on first. I never thought for one blooming minute she would, so, in some way, the whole idea of becoming a Chelsea Pensioner was just a bit of a joke.

After Christmas, I had to start making arrangements for Joan's cremation. It was the hardest thing I have ever had to do. The funeral director was a wonderful person and guided us through all aspects of the funeral. Joan and I had actually invested in funeral packages several years before so a lot of what I needed to get done was already catered for. All that was left for us to do was to include any personal touches that the family and I wanted, such as deciding that the coffin would be made of basketweave and that Joan would be buried in the gorgeous red dress she wore to Peter's wedding. The hardest part of the whole discussion was that I was aware that we were speaking about Joan as if she wasn't there any more and that made me so incredibly sad.

Next was deciding where to hold the service and who would officiate. Joan and I were not a particularly religious couple, but from time to time we would attend services at St Andrew's Church in the Thorpe St Andrew area. The vicar there was a wonderful woman, Darleen Plattin, whom we had got to know over the years and I could think of no one better than her to conduct the service. Not only was she a compelling speaker, but she also knew Joan well enough to be able to talk first-hand about her wonderful qualities. But there was a problem. When I called her, she informed me that she was currently away on a cruise and would only be returning to the UK the day *after* the planned date of the funeral.

'I'm so sorry,' she said during the call. 'I really wish I could be there to do it, but I just won't get back in time.'

Quietly crushed by the news, I breezily told her that I understood and that we'd make other arrangements. Secretly, however, I was absolutely devastated because in my mind Darleen was the only person for the job and I knew that Joan would really want her to do it.

For the next few days, I sought divine inspiration and then, out of the blue, it came in the form of a holy miracle phone call. It was Darleen. She was calling from the cruise and she had some news.

'Look, Colin. I have been thinking about it and I can't let either you or Joan down.' she said. 'I have cut my cruise short by a day and will be flying home in time to conduct the service.'

I was over the moon. 'Are you sure?' I asked, touched by the kind gesture.

'Of course,' she replied. 'I would really like to do it. For you, your family and for Joan.'

Now that was a real Christian woman, I thought to myself. What a lovely thing to do. The day before the cremation, the funeral director asked me if I wanted to see Joan one last time. I said yes, but when I arrived at the funeral parlour, I was suddenly filled with nerves. Why? I don't know. Throughout my lifetime I had seen many bodies, but this time, perhaps because this body belonged to the woman I loved, I felt uncomfortable. Did I really want to see her lying in her coffin? Or would I prefer to remember her in life, laughing and dancing the way she used to. I was torn. But I knew that this would be the last time I would see her physically. I had to say goodbye. She was the woman I had loved for 66 years. It was only fitting to send her on her way and tell her once again that I loved her.

I stepped into this dimly lit room where I could see Joan lying in her coffin, dressed immaculately in her gorgeous red dress. She looked beautiful, serene, just the way she used to look when she was sleeping. Her make-up had been done, her hair was beautifully styled, even her nails had been painted. Joan would have been very happy with the way she looked. I stared at her intently and said a few words, then kissed her goodbye for the very last time.

On the day of the cremation, I was astonished to see that there were so many people who had come to pay their respects. In fact, there were so many that some were unable to squeeze into the chapel and were forced to stand outside. Despite the lovely sunshine, it was a bitterly cold January day. Most of the mourners were old friends, family members, singers from the operatic society, friends from the gym and the various other places we'd frequented. I was pleased to see that everyone had taken note of the request in the invitations I had sent out, that instead of wearing sombre black on the day, they wear something yellow, Joan's favourite colour. My granddaughter Alice wore a beautiful yellow dress, while the pallbearers sported yellow ties. It was a lovely touch as I wanted everyone to remember Joan as the sunny lady we all knew and loved. As sad as it was, the wicker coffin looked beautiful with yellow ribbons and sunflowers adorning the sides. They reflected the real Joan with the sunshine smile. The ceremony was simple. Peter read out a beautiful eulogy for his mother and some lovely words written by Dawn and her husband Wajdi. I told the story of how we met. Darleen spoke beautifully about what a wonderful woman Joan was, and we played a piece of music by Jacqueline du Pré on the cello, which I knew Joan would love. One of the many extraordinary things about that day was the volume and quality of the singing, as the best of Norfolk had turned out for my wonderful Joan. All in all, it was a service that my darling would have been very happy with and it was the perfect send-off for the woman we all loved.

CHAPTER 34

Donning the Scarlets

When someone dies, it really is hard on the ones left behind. I was incredibly upset about losing Joan. I cannot describe how it feels to suddenly lose the person who has been standing beside you for the past 66 years. It doesn't register straightaway. For the first few days after she'd gone, there were so many times I expected to see her standing behind me or sitting in her armchair. Sometimes, something would happen and I would immediately think to myself, 'I must tell Joan.' Over time, it began to sink in that Joan was gone, but I was determined to make her live on in my mind. After all, why should I stop talking to her? Why should I stop telling her about what was going on in my life? It made me happy to feel like I was communicating with her, so I decided to make it a habit to talk to her picture every day and for her to continue to be a very important part of my life. That didn't mean I wasn't able to move on. On the contrary, I was very keen to start a whole new life. I knew Joan wasn't there any more and that life had to carry on.

After Joan was laid to rest, I set the wheels of change in motion, selling up the house and embarking on a new chapter. Dawn had the horrible job of sorting through Joan's clothes, which she found extremely emotional. Luckily, two of our friends were in the process of opening up a hospice charity shop and were in need of stock so we suggested they take anything they wanted. They were thrilled – and Joan would have loved this – because they thought she was a stylish, chic dresser and knew her pieces would go down a storm with customers. Although we felt guilty for giving away the dresses and suits Joan treasured, it actually felt liberating for us and helped in some way with the process of grieving.

Meanwhile, I gradually started to sell off bits and bobs from the house, such as furniture that I couldn't take with me. Someone who was looking after some student accommodation in the area approached me and snapped up all the cutlery, plates and bedding, so I managed to rehome everything. As a result, I ended up sleeping on a mattress downstairs for a little while before I did finally move on. I don't think I ever went upstairs again, except to shower. Eventually, the house became an empty shell and I began to look forward to moving to the Royal Hospital Chelsea. People say it is tough leaving a family home after many years, but even though the house in Norwich held so many dear memories, when I saw it stripped of everything, I realised it was just a house. The cherished memories associated with it will always live on in photographs, videos and my mind.

Although the idea of moving there started off as a bit of a laugh, the Royal Hospital Chelsea felt like the perfect place for me because it would mean I was nearer to my family – Dawn lived in north-east London and Peter lived in Surrey. I was still an independent chap who had a large circle of friends in Norwich, but at my age and with Joan no longer alive, I thought it was important that I stayed close to my family.

It took five months to confirm my place at the prestigious Royal Hospital Chelsea. To be eligible for admission as a Chelsea Pensioner, a candidate must be a former non-commissioned officer or soldier of the British Army who is over 65 and in receipt of either an Army Service Pension or a War Disability Pension or, as in my case, both.

I filled out a multitude of forms, sent them off and then waited. A few weeks later, I was offered a four-day stay at the Hospital. This was for me to decide if I felt it was the right place for me and for the officials at the Hospital to see whether I would fit in. I was allotted a berth for my stay, so I had the chance to get a feel for where I could potentially be living day to day. The term berth comes from the name for a cabin on a ship. The rooms in Chelsea are constructed from timber reclaimed from captured French warships. In fairness, I thought the berth was impressively sized for one soldier – it featured a small study area that led into a bedroom with an en-suite bathroom. It was a cosy set-up and perfect for living in. If I did fancy stretching my legs or popping out for a spot of fresh air, I had the rest of the Hospital to explore, with its wonderful architecture, designed by Sir Christopher Wren, and expansive grounds.

Over the next four days, I got to see how the Pensioners lived their lives at the Hospital and how much of a community there was, which warmed my heart. I got to look around the historic buildings and I dined in the magnificent Great Hall which, when you walk in, simply takes your breath away. With its high ceiling, wonderful wood panelling, run of huge windows along both sides of the hall and a huge mural of the Hospital's founder, King Charles II, the Great Hall still impresses me to this day.

I was then measured up for my Scarlets – the famous red uniform that is synonymous with the Chelsea Pensioners. It was only then I realised the true significance of living in a place like the Royal Hospital Chelsea. Becoming a Chelsea Pensioner was like joining an elite force of men. Not many get the chance and living there would be an honour and a privilege.

I must admit I felt at home straightaway and I was hoping I'd cut the mustard with the committee who would decide if I was the right fit for the Hospital. For one, the place reminded me of my years in the Army, living in a barracks, albeit a pretty fancy one. I liked the fact that I could be living among men and women who had been through similar experiences as me and had many stories to tell, whether it be about the adventures we'd been on with the Army or the loss of a loved one that may have led us to the Hospital. At 87, I was seeking that sense of community and the bond that you can only find with individuals who have gone through similar experiences to you.

A few weeks later, my place was confirmed. I was simply thrilled. I couldn't wait to slip into my very own Scarlets for the first time. It was such an exciting time for me. On the day of the move I was filled with excitement and a little trepidation. It felt like I was starting a new life at university, living away from home for the first time, though as a very mature student. I was allotted my berth and Peter and Dawn were there to help me settle in and we had lunch together. I think they could see that I was going to be happy in my new environment – I think they'd always been worried about how I'd cope after Joan passed. It was touch and go for a while. I admit there were times when I did struggle without her being there by my side, it was only natural. But I was lucky, because unlike so many older folks, I had my dear family around me to pull me through the dark times when I felt alone or when I yearned to be with Joan again.

After lunch, they settled me into my berth but, before they left, I handed Dawn my car keys and told her to take my car. She refused at first, but I explained, 'What do I need a car for? I have everything I need here.' I was just keen to offload all the superfluous things in my life – and also I didn't fancy the thought of London driving. All the important things I wanted were in my room, such as my military paraphernalia, my family photo albums, my TV and computer, and a beautiful large photograph of Joan, which had been taken at Peter's wedding and which now hung proudly on the wall opposite my bed. That's the picture I now speak to every morning and evening with my latest updates.

I settled into Hospital life pretty quickly and I was never bored. There are so many things to keep us busy – lots of organized events inside the Hospital and, if you are willing to participate, many official duties to volunteer for. There is something for everyone.

Every year the pensioners get the chance to take part in the Founder's Day parade, which takes place on a day around 29 May, the birth date of Charles II. Also known as Oak Apple Day, which refers to the oak tree that Charles hid in to avoid being captured by Parliamentary forces after the Battle of Worcester in 1651, this important event takes place within the grounds of the Hospital, with the gold statue of the King taking centre stage. The event has taken place almost every year since the founding of the Hospital in 1682 and is attended by a member of the Royal Family and around three-thousand of our nearest and dearest. In 2019 we were lucky enough to be joined by Prince Harry, Duke of Sussex, who managed to fit us in between changing nappies for his adorable baby, Archie. Sadly, he didn't have his beautiful wife Meghan with him, but it was an honour to be part of the parade in the year that marked the 75th anniversary of D-Day, and that was attended by such a respected member of the Royal Family.

Everyone at the Hospital was very friendly and welcoming and I seemed to fit in well. Oddly, I am still to come across anyone with whom I served during my own army years, but I have met many daughters and sons of people that I did know. Of course, there are people who served in the same regiment as me – the Gunners – but many years after. There are lots of great characters here who have seen the harsh sides of war, and there's a woman I frequently see around the gardens who was one of the code breakers at Bletchley Park. I have made a few friends at the Hospital, but only one or two close ones. For example, there's a lovely chap called Fred, who served with the Royal Tank Regiment and lives in a berth along from me, and we often have a drink together and chat about what life was like in the conflicts and wars we have been involved in, and what life was like afterwards as we adapted to normal life again.

There is also a lively social life to be had. Curry supper, which takes place on the last Friday of every month, is one of my favourite events of all and is a great chance for some of the boys to get together for drinks and a singsong. But there are a lot of chaps who live within the Hospital who simply like to keep themselves to themselves, preferring to stay in their berth or just go for a stroll around the grounds and say nothing more to anyone than a 'hello'. That's their prerogative, of course.

When I began to settle into the Hospital, I made sure that I always kept my mind and body alert. If I wasn't reading books and newspapers, I would continue to keep fit by visiting the onsite gym or going for brisk walks around the gardens. I also volunteered to sing at the Hospital's dementia ward. Major Philip Shannon, who had previously been director of music for the Irish Guards and Welsh Guards, leads the little band who perform songs for the patients every Thursday at eleven in the morning. I originally got involved with them when a lovely lady called Prue – a volunteer from outside the Hospital who plays piano with the band – asked me if I'd like to come along and sing with them. As you can imagine, I was only too happy to oblige. If I was able to sing, then I was very happy indeed and it was for a good cause – to bring some sunshine into people's lives. I've been doing this now for the past two years and I try not to let them down. It's almost magical to see the patients respond the way they do. Sometimes I might spy the tap of a foot or someone rocking from side to side to the music. It makes me feel so proud that we are reaching them in some way. It's a well-known medical fact that the brain responds to music, which is why music therapy is so important.

However, visiting the patients in the dementia ward also breaks my heart. I always get to the ward a little early (that's the soldier in me) and, while I wait for Prue to arrive for the sing-song, I watch the patients sitting around me and – God forgive me for saying it – I say a little prayer and plead, 'Please God, not me.' As we get older, we are afflicted with all sorts of illnesses. I've had heart attacks, I've lost Joan to cancer, all horrible experiences. But I find Alzheimer's and dementia frightening diseases that can devastate not only the patient, but also the poor family around them who must watch their loved ones slip into a vegetative state. It must be so traumatic for them to watch someone who was once so active and vibrant slowly fade away. Life can be so cruel sometimes and, in some ways, I am glad that Joan left me the way she did because I never had to watch her suffer.

It's nearly three years since Joan died and I have been at the Hospital for two and a half years and I really couldn't ask for a happier life. Well, I could. I would ask for Joan to be back in my life. But I realise what an opportunity I have had to become part of the the Royal Hospital's illustrious history.

I love slipping into my Scarlets, I feel so honoured to be one of the chosen few to wear them. Of course, we're not obliged to be in them all the time. They're heavy outfits. As Chelsea Pensioners, we are asked that we wear the scarlet uniform when we are representing the Royal Hospital in public or when on parade. So, for example, when I appeared on *Britain's Got Talent* I wore my uniform because I was representing the Hospital. Day to day, however, we wear a blue uniform, especially if taking breakfast or lunch in the Great Hall or roaming around the local area. We provide a service of sorts and it's truly heartwarming when people come up to us and ask for pictures or ask us questions about living at the Hospital or our time in the Army.

Being a Chelsea Pensioner is more than just being a former serviceman enjoying his or her twilight years in the beautiful grounds of the Royal Hospital. We represent every single man and woman who has ever served our King, Queen and country. I couldn't be prouder of representing the British Army. I might be biased, but I believe the British Army is the best in the world.

And to think that, once upon a time, just a stone's throw from where I live now, I was a tearaway with few prospects. Now I stand proud among my peers who have all helped to protect the values of the society we all cherish, in some small way.

PART 8

Britain's Got Talent

CHAPTER 35

Singing for Joan

So here we are. Where we started off. I still cannot believe that I won *Britain's Got Talent*. It's just not something that happens to people like me. I mean, I'm not exactly a wide-eyed teenager with stars in my eyes, my head in the clouds or a ferocious ambition to be famous. I'm a man of almost 90 who has pretty much lived his life and is happy to take things easy for now. Or am I? I'm not so sure. As you've seen from my story so far, I've never been afraid to take on challenges that seem beyond me. I clawed my way out of poverty-stricken Camden, overcame my educational difficulties to gain rank within the military, survived a terrible war and, perhaps my greatest and most fulfilling achievement of all, pursued the girl of my dreams and convinced her to marry me. So perhaps my taking part in *Britain's Got Talent* isn't such a stretch of the imagination, after all. As I always say, as long as you still have a pulse you might as well try your luck with life. Who says you have to stop dreaming when you reach a certain age?

If there's one thing I hope my triumph on the show has done, it is to prove that anything is possible at any age. It's never too late to dream or try something new. And that's what I did, although I must confess that I can't take full credit for my decision to apply.

It was actually an idea that was suggested to me by one of the old boys at our monthly curry suppers.

Every last Friday of the month, a bunch of us Chelsea Pensioners and a few staff members gather in the club room for what's known as curry supper. It's a splendid mix of hot, spicy cuisine, charming company and a good old-fashioned sing-song. As you can imagine, with my love of music, it is one of my favourite events in the Hospital calendar because after the meal I love nothing more than getting up and singing a few old favourites. One month, me and a mate, Bill Gorrie, were taking turns at putting on some entertainment. Bill was belting out some jaunty country music, while I was crooning some of my favourite old ballads. During a break in songs, I said to one of the fellas in the room that I was of the opinion that if you don't use your voice as you get older, you'll lose it. I went on to explain that that's why I enjoy singing at the curry suppers and in the Alzheimer's ward at the Hospital so much, because it keeps my voice in working order. At the end of the supper, as I was gathering my things together, before heading back to my berth, one of the boys strode up to me and said, 'If what you say is true and you like singing so much, why don't you go on that *Britain's Got Talent*?'

I laughed at him, thinking he was pulling my leg. 'How much have you had to drink?' I scoffed. 'Why on earth would they want an old man like me on the telly? It's a young person's show.'

'Who says?' the chap replied. 'Why don't you try it? In fact, I challenge you to do it.'

Thinking he must have consumed way too much vino during supper, I laughed it off again and bid the fella a fond farewell.

However, as I strolled through the impressive grounds of the Royal Hospital Chelsea, the suggestion frustratingly remained lodged in my mind. It was the most insane idea I had ever heard in my entire life, I kept telling myself. Me, an aged Chelsea Pensioner taking to the stage to try to outperform a bunch of youngsters on one of TV's highest-rated shows? The notion was just too ridiculous to even contemplate, no? Or was it? In fact, why shouldn't I try out for the show? I thought I had a little talent, which was more than could be said for many of the entrants Joan and I had seen over the years. And it had always been a dream of mine to perform on television, even if I had no ambition whatsoever to launch myself as a chart-topping crooner. By the time I had reached my berth, I had convinced myself to at least fire off an application, which I did. Then I sat on the edge of the bed, looked at Joan's portrait on the wall and talked the idea through with her. When she was alive, we used to watch the show a lot. We found it most entertaining, especially when those foolish acts who thought they were more talented than they actually were left the stage with their tails between their legs. However, in spite of our musical history at the operatic society, neither Joan nor I ever considered applying for the show because we didn't consider ourselves good enough

Now, however, I was captivated by the idea and felt I had everything to gain and nothing to lose. The worst that could happen, I said to her, was that I wouldn't hear back from the production team which, for me, was no big deal. But there *was* a wafer-thin chance that I might at least secure a first audition, which would be an achievement in itself. Beyond that, sailing through the various rounds, singing for Her Majesty The Queen at the Royal Variety Performance – it all seemed like an out-of-reach and thoroughly unrealistic fantasy.

As I climbed into bed I hoped that I could make it through to the first-round auditions so I could at least say I'd been on the telly. I was also hoping an appearance on the show could raise the profile of the Royal Hospital Chelsea and give viewers more of an insight into what we Pensioners are made of and all the good work that is done here.

A few weeks later, I received an email informing me that I had been invited to meet the producers for a first round of auditions that would take place at the ExCeL centre in east London. I was excited that there was some interest from the production team in seeing me, but was a little disappointed to discover that this was just a pre-show audition set up for the producers to determine whether or not I'd make the cut for the proper first round of auditions that you see on the TV.

When I arrived at ExCeL with my daughter Dawn and granddaughter Alice, I was shocked to see the number of people who were waiting in the queue to be seen. There were literally thousands and thousands of them, all bright faced and eager. I think I had naïvely believed that this early invite had been sent out to just a very lucky few hundred people. But from what I could see there were thousands of wannabes of every age, size and talent all crammed in together behind railings, waiting for their turn to shine and show producers what they'd got. For a moment, I asked myself, was I simply wasting my time? Surely the producers were looking for the next big thing, who had the potential to carve out a long and successful career. I was 89, for goodness sake. What were they going to do with an 89-year-old?

Once the snaking queue was whittled down and I made it through the doors, I was shown into a room where I sang a couple of songs for a panel of smiley-faced producers. They seemed to like what they heard and asked me to wait to be seen by yet another panel. I was impressed at how thorough this process was and then wondered why so many 'bad' acts made it through to the series. I realised, of course, that whether or not a young ambitious soul was talented or not, some people just made good TV.

Once I made it to the next room, I was asked once again to sing the songs I had prepared and talk about who I am, where I had been and what I was hoping to achieve from making it on the show. I told them about the challenge I had been set and how I had moved to the Royal Hospital Chelsea after the death of my wife, who would be so proud if I managed to make it onto the main show. I could almost see the producers' eyes light up as I shared my emotional story, but still they gave nothing away. Instead, they flashed me even brighter smiles than before and told me that I would hear in due course whether or not I would proceed any further.

I headed back to the Hospital feeling rather proud of myself. If this was as far as I had got, I would be happy. Getting this far was a worthy achievement. The fact that I had actually made the effort to apply was accomplishment enough. After all, how many of us just sit around and fantasise about doing things but do nothing about it?

A few weeks later I received a phone call from someone from *BGT* who told me the amazing news that I had been selected to audition for the celebrity judges at the London Palladium. While the idea of singing before a panel as knowledgeable about talent as Simon Cowell, Amanda Holden, David Walliams and Alesha Dixon was exciting enough, the chance to perform at the Palladium, even for five minutes, was a dream come true. It was the legendary venue that had hosted many of the world's greatest artists, such as Sammy Davis Jr, Max Bygraves, Bruce Forsyth, Judy Garland and many more. I couldn't believe what I was hearing. The person on the other end of the line furnished me with the dates, location and the suggestion that I perform in my Scarlets, but I wasn't really listening as I was too busy imagining myself bathed in a spotlight on the stage of the Palladium.

A few weeks later, there I was at the London Palladium at nine in the morning, looking smart in my Scarlets. I was supported that day, and every subsequent step of the way, by the brilliant Major Shannon, one of the senior officers in charge at the Royal Hospital. Much of the day was made up of doing on-camera interviews backstage and it wasn't until five o'clock that evening that I finally made it out on stage. When I did, I was raring to go. It might seem odd, but I felt no nerves, just an exhilarating wave of excitement.

As the delightful Ant and Dec ushered me onto the historic stage, the audience erupted into the warmest, most enthusiastic applause, which warmed my heart no end.

Taking centre stage, I looked around me and couldn't believe this was all real. There I was standing in front of a packed house on the same stage Frank Sinatra and Vera Lynn had once performed on. Whatever happened after today, I was happy in the knowledge that I had sung my heart out at the London Palladium. I still pinch myself when I think about it now.

The panel gave me an equally delightful welcome and David Walliams explained to his fellow judges that he and I had met before. A few months back, the hugely successful author had paid the Hospital a visit to meet some of the Pensioners for a new children's novel he was in the process of writing. He explained that it featured a Chelsea Pensioner and that he wanted to get a real feel for the way we lived day to day at the Hospital. We took David on a tour, during which he asked us about what it was like living in such a beautiful and celebrated historic building and what kind of things we did to busy ourselves with. He was a real gent and wonderfully funny, whipping us old fellas into hysterics with his funny asides. But that was months ago, so I was extremely touched that he actually remembered me after all this time.

Before I launched into my audition song, 'Wind Beneath My Wings', I explained to the panel and the audience that I was singing a song that was dedicated to my late wife, which garnered a huge 'awwww' from the crowd. I had the crowd behind me, I thought to myself. That's a good start.

As I launched into the song, I immediately sensed the audience was with me. The lyrics were so poignant for me and I think the people looking on could sense just how much they meant to me. When I reached the anthemic chorus, the audience burst into applause and it was clear the song choice had hit the right spot with everyone. But, as I carried on singing, the audience seemed to disappear and in their place I could see my heavenly Joan sitting in the seats looking back at me with her beautiful smile radiating like a spotlight. For the duration of the song, I directed each word at her as if I were dictating a love letter. When I reached the end of the song, Joan was no longer there and I was back in the room again as the audience let rip with their applause, while the judges jumped to their feet in appreciation.

I was glad it was over, but I had loved the experience so much that I would have been happy to sing another three or four songs. The judges were extraordinarily complimentary about my performance, with Simon spinning his well-used line, 'You are what *Britain's Got Talent* is about.'

When they gave me four 'yeses', I couldn't quite believe my ears. I was over the moon, of course, but I really hadn't expected to receive such glowing reviews.

Backstage, Ant and Dec congratulated me on getting through and gave me a warm hug, telling me they were looking forward to seeing me again at the semifinals. Just as I was about to leave, Simon and David suddenly appeared at my side, wearing the happiest of smiles.

'Colin, you have made me so happy,' Simon gushed. 'I wasn't really impressed with the standard so far today but seeing you on stage there and hearing your story has reminded me exactly why we do all of this, thank you.' Coming from him, that was wonderful praise indeed.

The audition had been filmed in January 2019 but was due to be screened when the series launched in April. To mark my episode, Dawn decided to throw a party and invited over some friends, family and neighbours to watch me in action. As the episode began, I was excited and a little curious to see how I would look on TV as they say that the camera adds weight. When the moment arrived, I must admit I was too moved by the way the production team had presented my story to worry about the way I looked. They had done it in such a sensitive and respectful way. It was a tough watch for the whole family as it took us back to that awful day on 19 December 2016 when Joan spread her wings and left us. After my performance, I took myself away from the party for the moment as the memories of that dreadful day came flooding back and I didn't want people to see that I was upset. But I pulled myself together and didn't stay sad for long because I knew that Joan would have been furious if I had. For the rest of the evening, tears were wiped away and instead we all got up and sang and danced and let loose, with Joan never far from our minds.

I'd forgotten that when a TV show airs, it's not just me watching it. Millions of other people have tuned in too, so you can imagine how amazed I was by the insane reactions I received online that night. Now, as you might guess, I'm no expert when it comes to things like Twitter or Facebook, so I happily relied on my social-media-savvy granddaughters, Ashley and Alice, to feed me regular updates on the reaction from the public. After the show, Alice proudly told me I was 'trending on Twitter'! Of course, I had no idea what she was talking about, but she assured me that it was something to be very proud of and that my performance had gone down a storm with people all around the world. Even TV tough man Piers Morgan had confessed I had made him cry. Well, I never!

I think it's safe to say that after the show, my life changed dramatically. I appeared on TV shows such as *Lorraine* and *This Morning* and I did interviews with magazines and newspapers. Yes, me! The reactions that I received from the public left me totally bewildered. Normally, when I'd venture outside of the Hospital in my Scarlets, tourists would approach me and ask me if I was a Chelsea Pensioner – or a Beefeater – and then request a selfie, which of course I would happily agree to. But now, after the show, people were dashing up to me and asking if I was that soldier chap from *Britain's Got Talent*. It was a very strange but heartwarming experience.

A few weeks later, the semifinals took place at the Eventim Apollo in London's Hammersmith. This time round, it was all change. The atmosphere backstage was much more frantic than my first audition. I guess the competitive aspect of the show was kicking in as we were all fighting for a place in the final at the end of the week. Don't get me wrong, there was an amazing camaraderie backstage – it actually reminded me a little of my army days. Everyone was supporting each other, but we were also aware that we all wanted to get through the next round and needed to put on a performance that secured that.

For the semifinal, I had chosen the old wartime classic, 'We'll Meet Again'. When I'd initially run the idea past the producers, they absolutely loved it and suggested that this time, as everything in the semifinal would be bigger and more outlandish than the previous audition, I would sing the track backed by some of my old Chelsea Pensioners. I thought it was a splendid idea and so the

Hospital roped in a bunch of other Pensioners to join me on stage. They were absolutely thrilled.

When we took to the stage, the audience's reactions were unlike anything I had ever experienced before. I felt like I was at a rock concert. Unlike at my first audition, everyone in the audience now seemed to know who I was and I could hear some of them shouting out my name. It was a rather extraordinary thing to hear.

Once again, the performance went down a storm and I was genuinely shocked when Ant and Dec announced at the end of the results show that I had made it through to the grand final. To think this had all started out as a tipsy challenge at curry supper and now, here I was, set to appear in front of more than ten-million viewers, hoping to scoop the title and all that went with it. It was simply madness, but winning would be a dream come true. I really couldn't get my head around the fact that an 89-year-old Chelsea Pensioner like me had beaten so many talented young people to secure a place in the final of one of Britain's most-loved shows.

The days leading up the final were a whirlwind of interviews, rehearsals and meetings but I was enjoying every single minute of it. It was such a remarkable contrast to the kind of things I would normally be doing at the Hospital and it was a real education.

Hours before the final show was due to start, the contestants did final camera rehearsals and I realised just how many talented people were hoping that a triumphant result would change their lives and futures beyond recognition. I wasn't sure what winning would do for me. I mean, fame was a young person's game, wasn't it? For many appearing on tonight's line-up, this would be their first proper step to success. There was Kojo Anim, the London comedian who was still waiting for his big break, the dashing and very clever magician Ben Hart, who was at the start of what looked like a very successful career, and then there was the madcap headmaster Mr McPartlin and the children from Flakefleet Primary School from the north-west of England, who had enchanted audiences with their chaotic musical performances. Of all the acts, this was probably the one that captivated me the most. I was moved by the bright-faced kids who couldn't believe what was happening to them and I had a lot of admiration for their headmaster, whom I sadly never got to meet. I thought he was simply incredible. He threw himself into every performance to make his kids happy. He dressed up for them, danced with them and it was clear that they absolutely adored him and would do anything for him. Their performance was complete and utter chaos, but I loved it nonetheless because I could see the children were having the time of their lives.

This time round I'd chosen the Andrew Lloyd Webber classic 'Love Changes Everything'. Once again, I would be backed by some friends from the Hospital as well as some young soldiers singing along in the aisles of the hall. The song worked its magic on the audience and when I hit that final note, red poppy leaves rained down across the auditorium and images of my Joan flashed up on big screens, the audience and judges jumped to their feet in an ovation that I will never forget. It took an effort for me not to shed a tear! The warm response from the thousands of people in front of me was most unexpected and gave me the greatest feeling I had experienced in a long time.

Later, the finalists were called back out on stage and the final three were called out. Because my hearing aid was playing up that evening because of the ferocity of the audience's reactions, I genuinely couldn't believe my ears that I was chosen as one of them, alongside Kojo and the remarkable Masked Magician, who had shocked the judges by revealing himself to be former contestant Marc Spelmann.

And then the tension really kicked in. Which of us had been voted the winner by the great British public? Watching it back, it didn't seem like much time had passed before Ant and Dec announced the result, but standing there in front of all those people it actually felt like hours before my name was called out. And even then, I didn't quite catch it because of my hearing aid. When I realised it was me, however, I was astonished. You can see from my face that I was certainly not expecting that outcome. My family still tease me to this day that they've never seen me pull that face before or, for that matter, since. Simon was obviously pretty pleased with the result too as he saluted me from the judge's desk.

All of a sudden, the audience began chanting my name and gold confetti filled the room. I wasn't quite sure what to make of what was going on. This was never really meant to happen, not to me anyway. But apparently it had. In case I'd forgotten, Ant or Dec reminded me that winning meant that I could look forward to receiving £250,000 and would be performing for the Royal Family at the upcoming Royal Variety Performance later in the year.

Unless something like this has happened to you, you will probably not appreciate how surreal it is to be at the centre of this mad storm. It's exhilarating but absolutely terrifying at the same time. I really was in complete and utter shock; it's a small miracle that I didn't end up having another heart attack.

Despite my joy, it broke my heart that Joan couldn't be here by my side, dancing in celebration in the gold confetti that fluttered all around me. But I knew how proud of me she would have been as she loved singing as much as I did. She would have loved all the pomp and ceremony, but would probably have told me at the same time to be careful not to let it go to my head. I also think she would have loved the fact that pictures of us together were flashed up during the performances, although I'm not so sure she would have approved of them being fifty feet high!

After the madness had begun to subside, it took me a while to work out what had just happened. It was extraordinary. I had just never contemplated it. But I soon discovered that winning the show was only the start of it.

I had a whole new and very unexpected career stretching out ahead of me. A couple of days later, I was assigned a management team who would deal with the business side of things, negotiating deals and making decisions, all with my approval. It surprised me to find out that there was a lot of interest in me, so thank goodness I had the team because they were able to juggle all sorts of projects and ensure that I could tackle them without burning out.

In the days following the final, I did the rounds of the TV and press and was given an itinerary of events I had been asked to appear at. I really was quite taken aback that so many people were interested in me. And then my management absolutely floored me when they casually announced one day that I would be recording an album with the hugely successful company Decca Records. Me? An album? I couldn't believe my ears. Who'd ever heard of an 89-year-old releasing a record? It was madness! Utter tomfoolery! But my manager, Professor Jonathan Shalit, assured me that an album of great emotional anthems, including the songs I'd performed on the show, would go down a storm with music fans. I had no reason to doubt him. He'd been in the business for years and was responsible for the careers of many of the most famous and successful people in Britain. When he later suggested that I would embark on a UK tour in 2020, I thought he had lost the plot. But Professor Shalit is a canny gentleman and I trusted him.

Being fired like a cannonball into the world of showbiz is a rather extraordinary experience. None of it seems real. Everyone is suddenly your friend and wants to know what you think about everything. Doors that were once firmly closed to you are opened to you, even if the week before no one knew who you were.

I was invited to record on *Songs of Praise* the same week I attended the TV Choice Awards, which was a really raucous affair, quite unlike *Songs of Praise*. That particular evening was a real eye-opener for an old man like me because all these people I kind of recognized off the telly were knocking back the drinks like they were going out of fashion and some of them – no names mentioned – were then splashed all across the papers the next day because of their behaviour.

However, the real highlight of the evening was when *BGT* was named Best Entertainment Show. I was seated at a table with one of the show's producers and my daughter Dawn and, as the result was read out, the producer nudged Dawn gently to tell me to put my hat on because he wanted me to go up on stage with him. Not only that, but when we got there I was asked to say a few words, which I of course did, commending the show's marvellous team who had looked after me so wonderfully. Later that month, I performed at the National Reality TV Awards and was awarded the Lifetime Achievement Award of 2019.

A few weeks after the end of *BGT*, I was invited to take part in *BGT The Champions*, a spin-off series that invited back many of its previous winners and most popular entrants from the UK and around the world. Paul Potts, the show's first-ever winner, came back, as did Collabro, Twist and Pulse, Stavros Flatley and many more. I didn't actually consider myself a champion at this point as I was just fresh from winning the last series but I was flattered to be asked back and so humbly accepted the invitation. Sadly, when it came to it, I failed to make it through to the final, but I had fun singing a rather gorgeous song called 'Supermarket Flowers' by Ed Sheeran.

Winning the £250,000 was an unbelievable treat. Hand on heart, I've never had so much money in my bank account in my entire life. But I have tried to be careful with it. People who interview me keep asking me what am I going to spend it on? A world cruise? A sports car? But I just laugh at them. What would I want with any of that at my age? I have kids and grandkids whom I want to help out and have given them all a little something. To see my nearest and dearest happy is way more important than spoiling myself with expensive luxuries.

Winning the money was of course a wonderful upside of being on the show but, for me, the main draw was to perform in front of the Royal Family and hopefully Her Majesty The Queen at the Royal Variety Performance at the Dominion Theatre in November. For a soldier who had served under the Queen for 25 years, this would be a dream come true. Throughout the show, I had always said to myself, if it actually happens, I would die happy. I can't imagine how I will feel if I do perform for Her Majesty, but I am sure I will feel humbled and honoured as I never have before. I owe a massive debt of gratitude to Simon Cowell and his amazing *BGT* team for making even the possibility of that dream come true. Her Majesty is a wonderful woman and long may she reign.

The Royal Family will always have a place in my heart and I'm pleased to see it is in good hands with the younger royals, Princes William and Harry. A lot of people my age criticize the new generation, but old traditions change and we just have to get used to that. If you don't move with the times, you will never develop or open your mind to new things. If my grandkids are anything to go by, I think the future is looking pretty good. My grandchildren have really inspired me over the years and introduced me to things that I wasn't used to and I am forever grateful for that.

Yes, the world is different to the way it used to be, but I think it actually is a better place because it is constantly evolving. If you think the world should stay still and never move, then you might as well close your eyes and die. Where would we be without computers and mobile phones? Some of us might not be able to get our heads around them, but they certainly make the world an easier place to live in. Age, to me, is just a number and I treat it with the contempt it deserves. We have to keep moving.

And while I'm on the subject of the modern world, I am often asked what I think about kids today. They are criticized constantly and branded as snowflakes or a waste of space. But I think that's unfair. There are so many young people who are striving to make the world a better place and we should be proud of them and not rush to put them down.

So what next? What lies ahead for Colin Thackery, *Britain's Got Talent* winner and recording artist (that still makes me chuckle)? Well, who knows? To be honest, I never expected any of this to have happened in the first place so I'm taking everything in my stride. I now have a reason to look ahead, embrace the future and think about doing things that I thought were impossible. Things are moving fast in this ever-changing world and I can't wait to see what's around the corner for me, my family and for the world.

And Joan will be right there with me, every step of the way.

Index

Acknowledgements

The writing of this book has been a wonderful experience and many, many people have been instrumental in its creation. In particular I would like to thank: my son Peter Thackery and my daughter-in-law Sue Kershaw; my daughter Dawn Musharafie and my granddaughters Alice and Ashley Musharafie, and grandson-in-law Jonny Davies; my sister-in-law Janina Kufluk-Thackery and my niece Elaine March. All these relatives have worked hard in making content suggestions, proofreading and fact checking. I would also like to thank Major P Shannon OBE, one of the senior staff at the Royal Hospital, who, as director of music, was with me every step of the way during the *BGT* process, and Annabel Williams, my fabulous singing coach. Thanks to all the other dedicated staff at the Royal Hospital and my friends at the Hospital who have supported me on stage and during my time at this great institution.

The Publishers would like to thank the following people for their hard work in making this book possible: Colin's family and friends, especially Peter Thackery, Dawn Musharafie, Sue Kershaw, Janina Kufluk-Thackery and Elaine March for their support and help with the manuscript; Christian Guiltenane for his tireless work on the text; the Royal Hospital Chelsea for being so accommodating and allowing the use of their uniforms on the cover; Jonathan Shalit for his skilful handling of the proposal at the outset and his support throughout; Ian Bloom for his amicable handling of the detail up front; and Naomi Everson for her help with scheduling and promotion.

Lastly, we'd like to thank Colin for sharing his incredible life story. His dedicated love of his wife Joan touched everyone who worked on the book and the success he's achieved late in life couldn't have happened to a nicer man.

Picture credits

All photographs © Thackerafies Limited 2019.

Now you've read his story, why not hear
the voice that won the nation's hearts?

Colin's first album
Love Changes Everything
is available now.

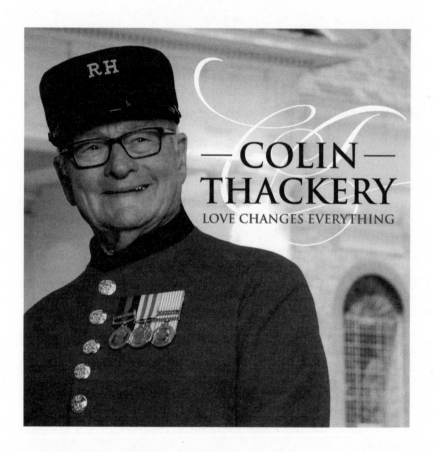

If you want to see Colin sing live, he is touring
the UK in 2020. Tickets can be found at
www.gigsandtours.com/tour/colin-thackery